Porch Perfect

Porch Perfect

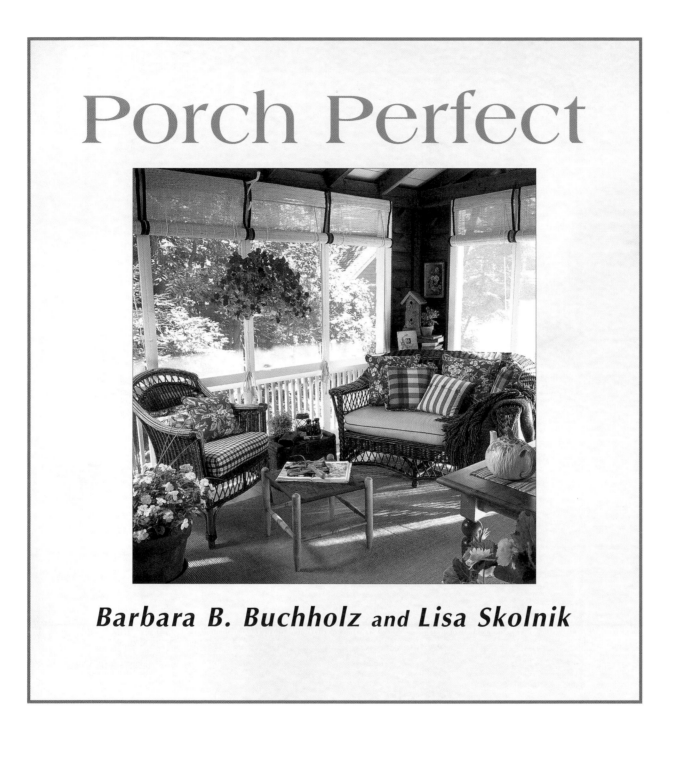

Barbara B. Buchholz *and* *Lisa Skolnik*

FRIEDMAN/FAIRFAX

PUBLISHERS

A FRIEDMAN/FAIRFAX BOOK

Library of Congress Cataloguing-in-Publication data.

Buchholz, Barbara Ballinger.
Porch perfect / by Barbara B. Buchholz and Lisa Skolnik
p. cm.
Includes bibliographical references and index.
ISBN 1-56799-772-4
1. Porches. 2. Architecture, Domestic—20th century.
I. Skolnik, Lisa. II. Title.
NA3070.B83 1999
728'.9—dc21 99-18741

Editors: Francine Hornberger and Reka Simonsen
Art Director: Jeff Batzli
Designer: Kirsten Wehmann Berger
Photography Editor: Wendy Missan
Production Director: Karen Matsu Greenberg

Color separations by Spectrum Pte Ltd
Printed in the United States of America

10 9 8 7 6 5 4 3 2 1

For bulk purchases and special sales, please contact:
Friedman/Fairfax Publishers
Attention: Sales Department
15 West 26th Street
New York, New York 10010
212/685-6610 FAX 212/685-1307

Visit our website:
http://www.metrobooks.com

To porches and patios: may the joy they bring our families be everlasting.

Thank you to the staff at Michael Friedman Publishing Group, particularly our tenacious and understanding editors, Francine Hornberger and Reka Simonsen. And thank you to Lucy Buchholz, who helped negotiate our technical difficulties.

Contents

Introduction   8

CHAPTER ONE
The Perfect Porch   32

CHAPTER TWO
Screened-In Spaces   46

CHAPTER THREE
All Glassed In   62

CHAPTER FOUR
Open to the World   92

CHAPTER FIVE
Special Places   116

Appendix   140

Sources   142

Index   144

Introduction

Close your eyes and picture a porch. Perhaps you conjure up an elegant white wooden Colonial house with a front gallery punctuated with stately Corinthian columns and filled with white wicker furniture. Maybe you see a frothy Victorian-era home framed by a wraparound veranda and loaded with elaborate gingerbread-style architectural elements articulated in a wide array of bright, exuberant colors.

Or do you imagine something much more contemporary—a streamlined concrete plane edged with low walls jutting off the side of a boxy concrete home and outfitted with massive sculptural furnishings? What about a wide redwood deck hugging the back of a low-slung ranch house that is completely open to sweeping views of a rolling yard with a swimming pool painted black to resemble a pond?

Try another fantasy: a screened porch that is off to the side of a house and furnished with leafy chintz-covered wrought-iron furniture and a ceiling fan offering comfortable protection from annoying bugs and the humid air. Or think of a glassed porch akin to a conservatory or orangery but for people rather than for plants.

The beauty of porches is that so many variations exist, both architecturally and stylistically, and none is more correct than another. While the first definition of a porch in *Webster's New World Dictionary* notes it as a covered entrance to a building, its second definition, that of an open or enclosed gallery or room attached to the outside of a building, is far more encompassing. This latter type of structure is also what has inspired countless homeowners throughout history.

Instead of simply building passageways to ease transitions between indoor and outdoor spaces, homeowners and design professionals have viewed the porch as an opportunity for an exterior room that can be built almost anywhere a structure allows. It can be attached to the front, side, or back of a house; be wrapped around the entire house; be built on the lower or upper levels; or it can even encompass multiple stories. It can be constructed of almost any material; be left open, covered, or enclosed; and can reflect any architectural style or period.

While it sometimes serves the primarily decorative purpose of creating an impressive entryway, a porch more often than not is used for active living, which is why its columns, rails, and pediments are embellished with decorative detailing rather than left bare, and why a whole genre of furniture has sprung up

OPPOSITE: *This lovely southern plantation house boasts a wraparound porch, perfect for enjoying refreshing breezes on sultry summer days. The earth tones employed on the porch create a segue between the interior of the house and the natural surroundings. A white wicker table and matching chairs serve up an alfresco breakfast, and twin rockers provide a place to relax and digest the meal.*

to turn these spaces into comfortable, practical rooms. Seating runs the gamut from wooden rockers and concrete benches to deeply upholstered wrought-iron and wicker sofas and chairs, as well as more minimal hammocks and swings. Other porch furniture has also taken hold, including tables made of wicker, glass, metal, and stone. The bottom line is that the options are endless.

In spite of the vast diversity of the porch's architecture and design, all these variations share common denominators: they encourage casual living, the enjoyment of nature, and interactions with the environment outside our doors.

The History of the Porch

Cave dwellers may not have had much time for leisure, but they nevertheless had the equivalent of small porches in the stone overhangs that extended from the tops of their caves and protected the grassy knolls or rocky stretches just outside their front "doors" or cave openings. These probably allowed them to interact with the outdoor areas in a way that would not have been possible if no structure were present.

Historically, the first true porches on record are probably the stately porticos of ancient Greek and Roman temples and public buildings. Referred to as a *porticus,* from which our own word *porch* derives, this formal roofed covering was supported by columns and intended to serve as a shelter from the rain and sun, and also as a pleasant transitional element between the outdoors and the inside of a building. In Greece a porticus stood at the front and rear entrances of a temple; in Rome, it was only at the front.

In Europe, outdoor spaces were used by both the poor and the rich. Royalty incorporated residential porches on their grounds for lavish warm-weather entertaining. At Versailles, Louis XIV's royal residence, landscape architect André Le Nôtre included formal courtyards, gardens with parterres, orangeries, and fountains. Peasants, on the other hand, were forced to entertain exclusively outdoors because their cramped homes generally consisted of only one or two rooms. Peasants fashioned outdoor dining spaces by hauling tables and chairs to the fields outside their homes, which set an early precedent for a space that assumed some of the functions of a porch.

In the United States, porches originated in two areas. Sir William Berkeley's home outside Jamestown, Virginia, built about 1640, had a porch on its upper level. John Carter's 1730s home, known as Shirley,

ABOVE: *Diverse styles are employed in porch architecture and design, but each one encourages its user to relax and enjoy nature.*
OPPOSITE: *In the mid-1800s, Greek Revival–style porches with columns were incorporated in southern mansions, sometimes encircling the entire home. In this example, the owners use both outdoor levels to sit, chat, and enjoy their colorful garden. And in summertime, the lower level could be a grand place to serve cocktails or hors d'oeuvres or set out a Sunday buffet luncheon.*

had a one-story portico, and Drayton Hall, the first Palladian house in this country, which was built in 1738 in Charleston, South Carolina, had a pedimented portico with columns.

Dutch settlers in the late seventeenth and early eighteenth centuries also built houses with porches. Their versions were called flying gutters because the roofs extended over the fronts and backs of the houses to provide protection for the entrances. When these overhangs were added to gambrel roofs around 1720, the front and rear verandas were born, adapted from homes in the French or West Indies, where the warm

ABOVE: *Even with architectural grandeur such as this, it only takes a few pieces of furniture to change the nature of a porch. Here, the majestic expanse of a sweeping veranda is made warm and practical with a simple table and chair.*

OPPOSITE: *Few architectural elements offer such an inviting welcome as a porch that spans the entire length of a house, as this covered wooden one does. A few rocking chairs, some pots of greenery, and a cold iced tea or lemonade are all that is needed for pleasant relaxation.*

climate dictated a need for an open living space to catch cool breezes, block strong sunlight, and protect occupants from sudden showers.

During the same period and for the same climatic reasons, porches became pervasive among southern homes and especially plantations. The Huguenots in South Carolina built porches on both sides of their houses so that neither façade was deemed more important. In the 1740s, French settlers in Louisiana built a porchlike *gallerie* around their raised cottage-style houses, which was also inspired by the architecture of the West Indies. Spanish settlers built porches and loggias on their residences in Florida, New Mexico, and Texas.

Many of the country's most illustrious citizens built porches of one sort or another, influencing the rest of the population. George Washington added a two-story porch with a colonnade at the back of Mount Vernon, his beloved Georgian-style home in Virginia. The former president wanted a place to sit and view the Potomac River and all its goings-on. The Georgian house of Henry Wadsworth Longfellow, in Cambridge, Massachusetts, was built with formal pilasters on the front and matching expansive pediment-covered porches on either side.

Thomas Jefferson, a renowned architect as well as a statesman, gave the façade of Monticello, his home in Charlottesville, Virginia, not one but a series of porches. The structure was his interpretation of what a functional residence should be, and he graced it with front and back porticos, a large forecourt with octagonal pavilions at the corners, and square pavilions terminating the wings. It was a carefully conceived adaptation of Palladian design that reflected Jefferson's personal architectural philosophy, and it made an important and enduring contribution to the popularity of the porch.

The massive Colonial and plantation houses of the Deep South in the United States contained one- or two-story galleries across their fronts that were supported with columns and hemmed in with shapely balustrades. A little to the north, Williamsburg styling was a bit more sedate, and a Colonial house of that region had a small porch based on classical temple portico forms with simple columns and pediments.

Georgian architecture, which first became popular in the United States in the mid-eighteenth century, celebrated the classical themes borrowed from the Italian Renaissance with exuberance, and the porches that accompanied such structures were equally elegant, sometimes bordering on grandiose. Though most Georgian houses were not very different from their Colonial forerunners, some reflected Palladian style with its ornate and lavish porches. Dayton Hall, built on the Ashley River near Charleston, South Carolina, in 1742 and still standing today, is considered one of the finest examples of full-blown Georgian architecture. It sports a broad double set of stone steps leading up to an imposing two-story pedimented porch.

After the American Revolution, Americans were eager to create their own vernacular style; they toned down their showy Georgian architecture just enough to create the Federal style, which was inspired by the

elegant work of British architect Robert Adam. The look became simpler and more streamlined, leaning toward sophisticated understatement; the proportions were exacting and more important than the ornamentation, which was less prominent than in Georgian residences. Adam developed a refined interpretation of decorative motifs from classical antiquity that became a major influence on residential architecture of the period. The porches that graced these Federal structures followed suit. Stately but spare Tuscan columns replaced ornate Corinthian versions; porticos lost the weight of massive pediments and became much more streamlined.

At the very same time that British styling influenced architecture in the New World, immigrants from Germany, France, Spain, Holland, Sweden, and other European countries built homes that reflected their ethnic traditions. From the end of the seventeenth century until the mid-nineteenth century, the distinctive looks they brought with them were incorporated into their residences as newcomers kept alive their traditions and shaped their new country's indigenous architecture. German settlers, for instance, brought their distinctive style first to Pennsylvania, Maryland, and Virginia in the eighteenth century, and another wave of German immigrants in the mid-nineteenth century made their mark in Texas, Wisconsin, and Missouri with structures based on the building traditions of their homeland. Porches reflected the architecture of their makers as each culture shaped them in its own distinctive way.

In both time periods the Germanic house was typically well built and efficient and had a steeply pitched roof. Most early versions were made of logs and had simple decklike porches, which were built from wood planks and had no balustrades. Homes made of stone, either left plain or whitewashed with plaster, were also popular, and these residences tended to be a bit more intricate, with small, squared-off porches in front of the entrance. Some of these homes also sported larger balconies that ran the length of the front of the residence and were always fenced in with balustrades.

Immigrants from Holland built steep, shingled roofs that jutted out over stone or shingled walls, forming some of the earliest and most elementary porches in the United States. Although eighteenth-century French Colonial–style dwellings in the Mississippi Valley were famed for their flared roofs and their galleries that encircled the entire house, their majestic porches actually stemmed from two separate influences. The pavilion, or steep central portion of the roof, was brought by French colonists from Quebec, where it had evolved from the thatched roof, while the gallerie came from the French West Indies. Spanish settlements that spread from Puerto Rico and Florida to the Southwest and the California coast incorporated courtyards and small *placitas* formed by lines of rooms, often fronted with *portales*, which were long, narrow rows of columns covered with roofs. These eventually led to the popularity of the recessed-style front porches in these communities.

ABOVE: *A rustic Adirondack summer cottage made of stone, logs, and twigs is graced with a porch that lends it provincial cachet, but is also sturdy and substantial enough to offer a shelter from the elements.*

OPPOSITE: *The porches that graced Federal homes were exacting, eloquently proportioned, and had streamlined Tuscan columns. This one gets lots of added charisma from a bold paint job that emphasizes the porch.*

OPPOSITE: *More often than not, a porch is used for practical living, which is why even the grandest versions are outfitted with functional furnishings. This large, elegant table is perfectly appropriate given the dramatic scale and stately nature of the space.* ABOVE: *Built-in banquettes with cushions provide an inviting place to stretch out on a stuccoed, columned porch. Some visitors might even fall asleep.*

Along the Gulf of Mexico and the Mississippi River, where one European power after another wrested control, cultures became intertwined. A blend of French, English, and Spanish influences is responsible for homes with hipped roofs topping galleries, one- or two-story galleries framed with balusters and columns, arcaded patios, and ornate wooden porches on homes made of adobe, frame, stucco, stone, shingle, or brick.

In the first half of the nineteenth century, Americans were captivated by all things Greek, thanks to the Greek War of Independence against the Turks, which was reminiscent of the American Revolution. Greece provided the inspiration for the predominant architectural style used in houses from 1830 to 1860, called at the time America's new national style. Now known as Greek Revival, the style reflects a strong affinity for the classical Greek temple, and the homes built in this mode are rife with dramatic, soaring porticos fronted with Doric or Ionic colonnades. Antebellum mansions in the South and frame or brick homes in the North, East, and Midwest all sported versions of the Greek Revival porch, ranging from prosaic to dramatic.

Later in the nineteenth century, and throughout the Victorian-influenced era that lasted from roughly 1860 to 1930, other trends gained favor along with Greek Revival, including Gothic Revival, Egyptian Revival, Moorish, and Italianate styles. Only the Gothic Revival and Italianate styles, both of which appealed to the romantic mood of the era with their picturesque appearances and ornamental diversity, came close in popularity to Greek Revival. Gothic Revival style spread rapidly throughout the United States all the way to the West Coast, and residences typically sported one-story entrance porches embellished with fanciful trims. At the same time, Italianate residences became equally common and usually had square entrance doors or towers placed off-center and flanked on either side with a piazza, or porch. Sometimes, a cast-iron balcony with Italianate ornamentation would front the second story of these residences, or a large Italianate porch might be topped with a balcony hemmed in by balustrades that ran the whole length of the porch.

Toward the last part of the nineteenth century and for almost the first half of the twentieth century, the Victorian style in all its incarnations took the country by storm. From Second Empire homes with mansard roofs, floor-length windows, and porches that spanned fronts of houses to the Queen Annes with round or faceted side towers sporting bays and turrets, steep-hipped roofs, and expansive wraparound verandas, Victorian residences gave new meaning and increased popularity to the porch. And regardless of the pedigree ascribed to a Victorian house, it was always paired with a splendid porch.

Along the Gulf of Mexico and the Mississippi River, French, English, and Spanish influences can be felt in arcaded patios. With furnishings in place, these structures become extensions of indoor living spaces. OPPOSITE. *An arcade with plenty of depth can become a full-scale living space with the addition of comfortable, durable furnishings.* ABOVE: *Use a space's natural assets. Here, the stone exterior of the structure also serves as the back for a series of benches that run the length of its gallery.*

In the Victorian era, many of the architectural styles that gained favor took their cues from abroad for the first time. Very different incarnations of the same Moorish theme are clearly evident in both of these spaces. ABOVE: This gracious residence was built with a grand loggia that adds to the building's architectural cachet. OPPOSITE: This porch, which makes a huge impact on its structure and actually lends it a specific style, was added after the structure was built and could work on many neutral façades.

Massive, rough-hewn stone Romanesque Revival homes of the period had recessed entrance porches with large, round arches, while Shingle-style Victorians often had enormous recessed entrance porches sporting Tuscan columns that wrapped around much of the front of the house, with another porch in back and decks off the home's second story. The highly picturesque Stick style, which was very popular by the 1860s, paid homage to the gingerbread chalets of the Alps and the half-timbered cottages of France and England, and spawned elaborate confections with deep overhanging eaves that were painted in brightly contrasting colors, ornamented with brackets and bargeboards, and studded with lacy openwork balconies and frothy galleries hemmed in with elaborate scroll-sawn railings.

Along with decorative detailing, the Victorian period eagerly promoted healthful living and outdoor pursuits. One offshoot of these ideals was the second-floor sleeping porch, which was used for napping or spending the entire night outdoors, sometimes even in cold weather. A tuberculosis epidemic and new information about how such diseases spread further encouraged the development of porches, since these concerns contributed to the desire for outdoor spaces and plenty of fresh air.

At about the same time that Victoriana gained favor, the most popular architectural style in the history of America to date, Colonial Revival, took hold, thanks to the centennial celebration in Philadelphia in 1876. With that style came myriad incarnations of the porch, from the simple arched pediment with narrow columns that came close to copying the original style to the ample verandas with eighteenth-century details that wrapped around homes and blended Colonial bones with Queen Anne detailing. Side porches with sash doors, thin columns, and balconies surrounded by balustrades became de rigueur on purist Colonial Revival homes.

Porches became much more commonplace for those who were less affluent after the Industrial Revolution freed homeowners from time-consuming tasks and increased the wealth of a great number of people. With more time and money, they had the chance to enjoy their families and homes, including their yards and outdoor living spaces. Advances in technology, such as balloon framing, also spurred the home-building trade and created a rash of new construction. Coupled with this, new pattern or plan books promoted an expanding pool of readily available housing styles, including many with porches.

ABOVE: *A porch doesn't necessarily have to match the vernacular of a house. Here, a red brick Colonial home gets a masonry-style Gothic Revival colonnade as a side porch off its dining room. Executed in stone and equipped with an informal dining set, it becomes important from both an architectural and functional standpoint.* OPPOSITE: *This Queen Anne porch is resplendent in its patterned shingles, turned spindle-style columns, scalloped brackets, intricate sawn railings, and exuberant color scheme.*

OPPOSITE: *The deck of a contemporary frame home gets a dose of Victorian styling with elaborate columns capped by an equally ornate entablature. This complicated design works well, thanks to the simplicity of the structure and the pared down decor of the deck.* ABOVE: *The owners of this lovely Victorian home have made the most of their wraparound porch by incorporating colorful details. The bright white balusters and porch supports—accented with just a touch of blue—show up well against the blue of the house's exterior, and cheery yellow wicker rockers provide a relaxing place to sit and enjoy the flowers that hang from the ceiling.*

In the early part of the twentieth century, the Arts and Crafts movement also spread throughout the country, mostly in response to a middle-class demand for affordable, efficient, and attractive housing. Though many regional variations developed, the most prevalent type of home associated with this style was the Craftsman bungalow, popularized by furniture maker Gustav Stickley. His magazine *The Craftsman* advertised his company's line of simple, well-constructed furniture, and in the publication he also printed free plans for suitable homes to house his furnishings. He hired architects to design these plans (they remained nameless) and offered more than two hundred free designs in all, which greatly helped to popularize the style. The resulting low-slung structures were usually long and shingled, had gabled roofs with wide overhangs and exposed eaves, and featured ample porches, as well as pergolas at the rear of the residences.

About the same time, Chicagoan Frank Lloyd Wright developed a new architectural style that did not owe its inspiration to any European form. Called the Prairie School, it was the beginning of modern architecture as we know it today. The houses that typified this style had some traits in common with Stickley's Craftsman bungalows: simple lines, functional floor plans, the integration of the house with the environment, and an emphasis on horizontal lines and wide eaves. Prairie houses also skillfully incorporated outdoor spaces that were natural extensions of the interiors, such as long, low porches under wide eaves either in the front or on the sides of the homes.

In the Spanish-influenced Southwest and West, Mission-style houses gained arched arcades. Prairie houses, which strove to integrate the inner and outer spaces of a home, incorporated several porches and terraces in their long horizontal sweeps, usually with overhangs from projecting eaves on the floor above or a hipped roof topping the structure. Frank Lloyd Wright's International style, which had grown out of the Prairie style, introduced poured-concrete, cantilevered terraces in such homes as Fallingwater, which is outside Pittsburgh, Pennsylvania.

Both the Craftsman and Prairie styles influenced a large body of working-class homes in the early twentieth century that are known today as homesteads, four-squares, bungalows, and cottages. If not immediately identifiable, they are simply called builder-style homes. Developers helped popularize these simple, affordable homes, as did publishers of affordable plan books and mail-order houses. Though the individual details of each type of home varied, almost every house had a front porch, offering its occupants the sort of interaction with their neighbors that fostered the growth of communities.

Many of these houses had a row of front steps known as a stoop (derived from the Dutch *stoep*), which served the same purpose as a porch, while others were embellished with full-blown porches as a way of garnering additional architectural significance, not to mention additional square footage. In fact, the porch became an important gathering place in these emerging neighborhoods. The classic front porch was a place to meet and greet neighbors or just to be seen and to see.

While nostalgic styles came and went through much of the twentieth century and continue to do so to this day, two new styles developed based on architectural developments on both sides of the Atlantic: the Art Deco or Moderne style, which was based on a streamlined aesthetic inspired by the machine age, and the International style, so called because it had roots in several European countries, including Germany, Austria, France,

ABOVE: *Clearly, a porch can raise the architectural quotient of a home. Here, the modest porch of a bungalow becomes more than the sum of its parts, thanks to the astute and subtle use of ornamentation. A lattice-work partition gives the space depth, while a contrasting color on routine architectural details makes them seem more significant and impressive.* OPPOSITE: *With outdoor pursuits enjoying a resurgence, a porch allows homeowners to incorporate simple elements of outdoor living—such as alfresco dining— into their lifestyles.*

Denmark, and Holland. Though neither style ever stole the hearts of the American public in the same way that Colonial Revival or Victorian structures have, they were important architectural movements that gave new dimensions to the porch. No longer spaces that wrapped or hugged a house from the outside, porches were architecturally integrated into the structure of the residence. A Deco home might have had a garden room made of glass block; a Modernist house might have been surrounded by a pavilion or flanked by concrete planes that served the same function as decks or porches.

After World War II, modern boxes with low-slung roofs and cantilevered spaces, known as ranches or split-levels, cropped up rapidly to meet the housing demands of returning veterans and their new families, who were moving to the burgeoning suburbs. In both forms, traditional decorative elements, such as a long, ground-level front porch tucked under the hipped roof, softened the basic silhouette of the home.

Though the porch went in and out of favor during this period, it has come back with a vengeance in the last decade or so, as the home has become an important refuge for most of us and communities have come to view their turfs as defensible spaces that need the attention of all residents in the area. The vistas a porch affords its owners of the surrounding environs are known to be invaluable for social and safety considerations. All porches share an ability to let their occupants relate to the world outside their homes. Some also add another dimension to their residents' lives by giving them more space, air, and sunlight, and an ability to increase the architectural cachet of their homes with a fairly simple basic design.

Homeowners are also reviving the porch because it can raise the architectural quotient of their residences, both for their own enjoyment and for resale value. The form a porch takes can match the style of an existing structure, enhance it with a composition that strengthens a particular motif, or completely change it with a spectacular new and different design. It can also become the equivalent of building an addition if the space is mined to its fullest extent. For instance, a screened-in porch outfitted with a dining set as well as comfortable seating arrangements can function as another family room in milder weather.

Furthermore, the porch appeals to a renewed interest in neighborhoods and the reawakening of a sense of community among homeowners, long promoted by such urban advocates as Jane Jacobs. More emphasis than ever is placed on reclaiming the residential areas of the cities we live in and making them safe. The age-old front porch allows us to monitor virtually everything that happens on a street.

In the suburbs the porch's main purpose may not be safety, yet it still has an impact on a person's and an area's sense of community. Neighbors actually get to know one another, thanks to the sociable habit of sitting and relaxing on the porch.

Evidence that porches are making a comeback is rampant. At the planned community of Seaside, a resort development in the Florida Panhandle that was started in the 1980s, every house must have a front porch. The porches must also be of a specific size (which is fairly large) and be constructed at set distances from the sidewalks—close enough so that these structures serve as a catalyst for residents and pedestrians to mingle. Of course, many of the houses also incorporate side porches, wraparound porches, back porches, and second-floor porches, and the eighty-acre (32ha) Seaside site is also rife with gazebos, mini piazzas, widow's walks, towers, and cupolas.

Seaside, whose slogan is "The New Town. The Old Ways," is considered an important model for the direction of land development in the twenty-first century, and the concept is being implemented in other communities and developments, both urban and suburban, across the United States. Town houses that line city streets even in cold climates such as Chicago have porches that hug the streets, and once-faceless suburban homes now have "eyes and ears" open to their streets because of porches that grace their façades. Individual homeowners incorporate porches into new homes or renovate existing homes to include porches for the same reasons: neighbors want to know one another, and the only way to accomplish that is by seeing and being seen on a regular basis.

Even apartment dwellers want to get in on the act. The lust for the great outdoors has increased the demand for balconies, a type of porch that extends from the walls of a building and is enclosed by railings. Though the impact of these spaces is much different for the apartment dweller, some facets are the same. Balconies can increase living space, provide a view, and allow immediate access to the outside, factors that must be extremely important since—according to builders and developers—the demand for this feature is so high. Even in harsh climates with devastating winters, apartment owners want their version of a porch, no matter how small and how infrequently they get to use it.

Thus the age-old porch remains popular, and is considered anything but old. It holds as much promise and meaning for homeowners today as it did when it was first added to our architectural vernacular—perhaps even more now that a premium on space and the high cost of building and remodeling dictate careful consideration of all our choices.

This book presents many examples of residences that illustrate the importance of the porch. Here you will learn how to create relaxing, inviting, and functional porch spaces of your own. Discover the numerous variations of the porch and the important creature comforts—such as tables, chairs, sofas, swings, and plants—that can personalize and beautify your porch.

OPPOSITE: *An otherwise unusable urban rooftop becomes a lush garden-cum-porch with the addition of wood planks for flooring and a wooden side railing. When you select plants for outdoor use, be sure that they're appropriate for your climate.*

CHAPTER ONE

The Perfect Porch

By its very definition, the word *perfection* implies superiority. While dozens of architectural styles dot the urban and suburban landscapes of the world, it is a matter of individual taste whether one is better than another. None can be considered the perfect style for a home. Similarly, no style of porch is more predominant or correct than any other, for like the structures they grace, porches come in many incarnations. A porch can be mammoth or minute, open or enclosed, gallery-style or wraparound, fanciful or functional.

In fact, there are porches to match, enhance, or merely grace every architectural style imaginable. Some porches were—and are—designed hand in hand with the structures they hug, embodying the same vernacular. But others completely change the nature of the rest of the house, differing dramatically from the existing architecture and sometimes looking almost tacked on.

Adding a Porch

Adding a porch to a house, whether from the moment it's constructed or later on, requires careful planning. A porch can fulfill many functions. It can be used as additional living space and assume the role of an adjunct sitting, living, or dining room, or it can be fitted for a very specific activity such as exercising, sleeping, or pursuing hobbies. Each of these roles affects where the porch should be placed and how it should be constructed.

Though there are no absolute rules about how to design a porch and where it should be placed, ideally it should harmonize with the architectural style of the house. It may match the existent architectural detailing or even add architectural interest and balance to a façade that is lacking. The bottom line is to determine what kind of porch will be most appropriate for the home and your needs. An architecturally significant older home, for example, should have a porch that closely corresponds to its particular style, while a generic structure can garner some architectural pizzazz with the addition of a portico and columns or a full-scale porch that spans the entire façade and is edged with a fanciful balustrade.

A porch should also be constructed of materials that correlate to the materials already used in the home's construction and that consider the property's orientation, its vistas, and the topography of the site. While porches help shade the rooms that they extend from, they can also darken those interior

OPPOSITE: A trio of Shaker-style rockers complements the spare, classic architectural elements and color scheme of this clapboard home in a Federal vein, and turns the porch into a spare room adequate for greeting neighbors or meeting with friends. Place the rockers in a row facing the street to invite neighborliness; move them close together when guests are present to create ambience.

rooms and obstruct the views. Depending on the materials used, porches can be either public or private spaces. Consequently, factors such as how the porch will be used and where it will be located should be weighed carefully.

While a generic porch can immeasurably increase the enjoyment a homeowner can gain from his or her residence, it will fulfill a different function if placed in the front of the home overlooking the street than if located at the side, where it will be far more secluded. A sleeping porch would be most appropriately located on the second story of a home, while the rear of a house would probably be most suitable for a porch intended to accommodate a home gym or hobby studio. Pick and choose the locale of a porch judiciously after considering all the ways you plan to use it.

OPPOSITE: *The shingled façade and unfinished plank flooring soften the elegant white balustrade and pillars of this porch. Vintage rush-seat add to the rustic feeling.*

ABOVE: *A straightforward frame house is given architectural drama and a striking off-center entrance with an angled portico jutting out from the corner of a wraparound porch.*

FLOORING MATERIALS

A porch, especially one that is open to the elements, demands a hard-wearing floor. The key to choosing a flooring material is determining what kind of wear and tear the porch will receive from users and from the elements. Following are some guidelines to heed.

OPEN OR PARTIALLY OPEN AREAS

Concrete, brick, tile, flagstone, and wood will work well for these spaces, and can also be used on covered porches or sunrooms.

Concrete is a simple, affordable flooring solution that can take on any shape or thickness and forms a cold-, heat-, and scratch-resistant floor. It can also be employed decoratively if you lay it in tiles, pack it like clay, add texture or pigment dyes, or finish it off with wax, paint, stain, or an acid wash. It should be sealed to make it impervious to water and stains.

Brick costs about the same as ceramic tile and can be found prefinished with glaze to protect it from staining. It's also available in different thicknesses and weights, and recycled bricks from salvage yards that are already worn with a warm, aged finish can be used on sturdier subfloors. Bricks can be arranged in a variety of decorative patterns and should be laid on a moisture-proof base, then sealed.

Tile is hard-wearing, easy to clean, immune to water and most household chemicals, heat-resistant, and comes in hundreds of styles. However, some tiles can be expensive, and installation often costs more than the tiles themselves. Terra-cotta, ceramic, and quarry tiles are naturally non-slip and won't burn, blister, or discolor, but all have their pros and cons.

Terra-cotta tiles, which are made from extruded or hand-formed clay, have a rich patina that looks great, wears well, and seems impervious to dirt, but these are relatively soft tiles that must be sealed with linseed oil and waxed for protection.

Ceramic tiles are made from dust-pressed clay fired at high temperatures and are the most waterproof type of tile. Those that are intended for use on floors are not glazed (unless the glaze has a roughened surface) because this would make them too slippery, and they are thinner and more uniform than terra-cotta or quarry tiles, which makes installation easier.

Quarry tiles are made from extruded or hand-formed clay that is fired at higher temperatures than terra-cotta to make them more durable, hard-wearing, and waterproof. Some mosaics are also suitable if made from ceramic or terra-cotta rather than from glass or marble tiles. Glass tiles are too slippery and fragile, and high-gloss tiles have smooth surfaces that mark easily.

Flagstone is a beautiful, versatile metamorphic rock formed from shale, and it is named after the process of "flagging," or the slicing of the stone into thin slabs. It comes in many colors, varieties, shapes, and sizes and usually costs less than ceramic tiles but is often more expensive to install. The two most common types of flagstone are bluestone and slate. Some varieties are porous and can be sealed and/or waxed; less porous varieties cannot be sealed.

OPPOSITE: *Bricks can be arranged in a variety of attractive patterns to enhance the decorative aspects of a space. Here, pavers are set in a very basic L-shaped configuration that adds just the right touch of rustic appeal to the loggia.*

Wood comes in many varieties and makes a very versatile flooring material, thanks to the new penetrating sealers and preservatives that are available today. Hardwoods and softwoods can both be used outdoors, but hardwoods are less likely to dent over time.

Sawn lumber is most appropriate for outdoor use, but it should be pressure-treated with a preservative that will penetrate deeply into its cellular structure to resist decay and termites. Exterior finishes such as water repellents, stains, and oils can also enhance the weathering abilities and durability of various woods.

Selecting the right wood is a matter of preference and budget, and also depends on other factors such as the indigenous species in each region (which can often be less costly) and grade. Several grades of a particular wood are usually available, ranging from those punctuated with knots to those that are smooth and knot-free. To help control costs, consider several alternatives, such as reasonably priced yellow poplar instead of expensive oak

OPPOSITE: *Tile is durable, water-resistant, easy to clean, and comes in hundreds of styles. Even a simple pattern can be used in an eye-catching and creative manner. These plain, square tiles are set on the diagonal for a more interesting effect.*

for a hardwood floor. Or choose thinner boards, planks, or strips that can be used to create diagonal, square, herringbone, and parquet patterns.

ENCLOSED PORCHES AND SUNROOMS
Virtually any surface can work here, including those mentioned above, but some are better than others. Easy-care alternatives include vinyl, rubber, linoleum, and cork.

Vinyl, made from polyvinyl chloride, is a tough and flexible plastic material that comes in various thicknesses and can incorporate many colors for a streaked, marbled, or glittery appearance. These effects are achieved with layers that contain different flecks of color, which can also be manipulated to emulate natural materials such as marble or wood. The surface is usually smooth, but can be textured for greater slip resistance. This low-maintenance, hard-wearing flooring can also be cut and inlaid.

Rubber can be made from both synthetic and natural materials, with fillers and pigments added for color and body. It's extremely hard-wearing, durable, and easy to clean. It's slightly softer and more flexible than vinyl, and the surface can be smooth, studded, or ribbed for slip resistance, which also gives the material a decorative quality. Rubber is available in a

wide range of colors and textured looks that appear marbled or granular.

Linoleum is a completely natural product with good environmental credentials since it is made from linseed oil combined with organic fillers such as wood, flour, or chalk. The ingredients are mixed into a paste with colored pigment, rolled into sheets with a burlap or fiberglass backing, then baked for three weeks. The resulting material is versatile, available in a variety of hues (some quite contemporary and light-years from what your grandparents or parents may have had), and can be inlaid. One downside: it shows marks easily.

Cork is a natural product made from the bark of the cork oak tree, making it durable, economical, and an excellent insulator and sound barrier. Always warm to the touch, cork is available in sheets or tiles of various thicknesses that are prefinished with varnish, left plain, or laminated. Unfinished tiles need to be sealed after installation; the laminated version is particularly hard-wearing and maintenance-free. Cork can also be used as an underlay for other types of flooring.

MAKING PLANS

Don't rush into the process of building your porch. It's important to take the time to determine what type of porch will best suit your needs and where it should be built. Start by making a wish list of all the functions you would like the space to fulfill. Once you have an idea of how you will use it, consider its location.

Though you may want it to be bright and airy, in this day and age too much light can be a detriment because it can make the space hot and much too susceptible to harmful ultraviolet rays. Consider siting the porch where it will receive some indirect light or shade for at least part of the day. Also consider whether you want it to be an open space or an enclosed one that can be used when the weather is less than ideal. Devices such as skylights or screening can be added to open spaces to increase usability. If your budget is limited and you'd like something substantial, consider an open porch that can eventually be converted to a year-round sunroom.

When you have a good idea of what you want, consult local contractors, who should be familiar with the building codes in your community and can give ballpark figures on the costs of both materials and labor. Get at least three suggestions and bids from contractors before you make your final decision so that you'll have the widest possible selection and a range of prices. You'll also probably have a clearer idea by then whether you want to call in an interior designer or architect to fine-tune the suggestions. Finally, always be sure you can work comfortably with your contractor, designer, or architect—compatibility is essential.

FITTING IT OUT

Once a porch or outdoor room is in place, fitting it out has a large impact on both how it looks and how serviceable the space will actually be. It's important to employ the same principles of interior design that apply to an indoor space. Furniture should suit the activities you want to enjoy in the space, such as dining or conversation. This means that seating should be grouped together in one part of the room, or a table and chairs should be carefully placed away from traffic patterns so that occupants can sit down and enjoy a meal.

Here are some pointers to keep in mind when decorating a porch.

TRAFFIC PATTERNS. Most porches double as entries or exits to a home, so be sure to allow for the flow of traffic when arranging furniture. Keep a clear pathway from the door of a home to the door of the actual porch so that nobody trips over chairs or has to walk around tables or sofas for access.

VIEWS. With any outdoor room, garden, or sunroom, what lies beyond the boundaries is often just as important as what lies within—if not more so. On a porch or in a glassed room with spectacular views beyond, place furnishings to take advantage of the scenery outside.

PRIVACY. Control the degree of privacy with blinds, curtains, and the arrangement of furnishings. If you want the front porch to embrace the neighborhood, keep it open and arrange the furniture to face the street; line up benches, rockers, or chairs in a friendly row. If privacy is more important than relating to the neighbors, put up a visual barrier of mesh screening, lattice, fabric, or vegetation and arrange furnishings in tight groupings facing each other instead of in wide-open arrangements that face the outside.

PORCH-FRIENDLY PIECES. For outdoor areas, pick furnishings made of sturdy materials such as treated woods, plastics, rustproof metals, and fiberglass that will withstand the elements but still be comfortable and attractive. For covered or indoor areas, furnishings can be adapted to the environment with an extra coat of paint or mildew-resistant fabrics or fillings.

OPPOSITE: *Structures that fulfill the functions of a porch come in myriad incarnations, such as this deck. Fitted out with umbrellas for shade and several places to relax with a cool drink, it operates much the same way as a porch.* ABOVE: *This stucco four-square would be prosaic and plain without its porch, which is sussied up with dazzling flowers instead of architectural elements.*

PORCHES

BY RICHARD R. RADTKE

(ORIGINALLY PUBLISHED IN THE *CHEROKEE DAILY TIMES* MARCH 7, 1996)

New homes never seem to have the grand old porches of yesteryear, the ones that reach out from the front of the home like a beckoning hand bidding welcome to all who come, and which have two old rockers, a porch swing, and perhaps a table or two. No, today, all you seem to see is a small unfriendly concrete slab, no chairs, no swing, just a slab in front of the door. I find this sad, their passing, and as a contractor I know it's a question of economics, combined with the

extension of the idea that a home should not have any wasted space. Though how anyone could call a porch wasted space is beyond me. There is no better place to watch the rain tumble down in sheets, or to feel the evening's gentle breeze. Where else could you watch the neighbor mow his lawn, or chat with the lady next door? It was the perfect place to watch the world go by and feel safe and secure.

I grew up in an old home with a large porch blossoming from the front, as long as the house was wide, bigger in fact than most of the rooms in the house. As children, we would jump from its side to the ground below, that is, until either Mom or Dad saw us through the window and put a stop to it with the cry, "What are you kids trying to do? Break your legs?" Then all jumps were suspended until they were out of sight. On rainy days, we would play on its floor,

listening as the thunder boomed overhead, watching as lightning danced in the sky. My father put a porch swing on that old porch some twenty years ago and there it still hangs, swinging back and forth, back and forth, as with it the wind is gently playing. Many a cool summer evening we spent on the porch, conversation our entertainment, no rush, no television, just the cool breeze and the sinking sun. My mother still lives in the old family home, and we visit her often. When the weather is just right and the sun begins to sink, the porch and the swing still call.

The old house my own family lives in today has an old porch. It juts out from the side of the house, off the kitchen overlooking the fields and opening to the eastern sky. The old-fashioned columns

LEFT: *It often takes just a little bit of creativity to make a plain porch much more interesting. The simple portico that spans the front of this house gets dressed up with the corn husks and pumpkins of early autumn.* OPPOSITE: *A cushioned porch swing and a profusion of vibrant flowers make this cozy front porch the ideal spot for relaxing with a good book or perhaps taking a nap under the vintage crazy quilt.*

that support the roof were delicately turned on a spinning lathe. The paint hangs on their curves in a halfhearted way, chalky and discolored with age, the surface weathered and cracked from one too many Midwestern winters. There is no railing around the old porch to keep out the wind, which pirouettes with dead leaves and debris in a whirling waltz, danced to the tune of an uplifting rush. This old porch is a comfortable place, like an old sweater or slippers or a pipe. It groans and shifts like an old man and suggests days and memories gone by.

In the morning on the old porch you sit, after first wiping the dew off a chair. Sit with a steaming cup of coffee to watch and wait for the sun to light its way into the morning sky, pushing back the covering darkness of night as it slowly ascends to its throne in the Olympian heights. The morning breezes blow through the fields of corn that fill the land, causing them to undulate like the waves of the sea. Birds, restless from the night, now with the light of the new day seek the freedom of the sky and fill it with their song. The cycle begins anew and holds promise.

As the evening approaches we sit on the old side porch and watch the lights of the town sinking on the horizon, the steady yet persistent flicker of the red light perched on the top of the grain elevator that juts up into the darkened sky. Lights

glow from passing cars and trucks as they rush along the highway. But though they are in sight, they are still far away, and we sit . . . isolated . . . and find comfort in that. There is no noise like that of the city; the symphony that plays here is that of silence . . . the gentle rustle of the wind as it plays in the grove, rustling leaves and swaying the tall grass in its wake, the rushing of the creek at the bottom of the hill.

It's easy to detach yourself from the rest of the world out there and just relax on the porch and ponder. Lean back in the creaking chair and think about nothing and everything, plan for tomorrow, and wish for yesterday. At times we watch the glow of the passing cars as they move

across the horizon and imagine where they are going and why. To Grandma's? To work? Perhaps, to visit a sick friend? Who knows?

Above us an untold number of stars blaze in the night sky. We count them one at a time. The nebulous band of the Milky Way cuts a swath among them and through them and if you watch long enough you are destined to see a falling star, spitting and sputtering as it plummets down from its heavenly home. The child inside you makes a silent wish while the adult that you are just sits and stares. When the moon is full, a glowing white disk shadow dances in its pale light and the darkness never really arrives. So you just sit . . . and rock in your chair.

Letter from the Porch

I was greeted with a letter today from someone whom I have never met, although perhaps some day I may. It was a wonderful letter, written with care, full of memories and sprinkled with tears. The author wrote of the porches and homes that she had known since her childhood. She wrote bits and pieces from the past, weaving them all into a tapestry of life that was full and true. The words that she used were just words, but through them the pulse of the emotions that lay beyond came through. The stories she told were hers and hers alone, each in turn, which have been told before and will be told again. Each one of them is common to all of us in some way. The bits and pieces that she wrote spoke with nostalgia of love in the spring and the growth that summer brings. They were the words of a neighbor sitting on a porch as the setting sun finds the solace of rest behind the faraway horizon.

She talked of long-ago nights when the summer breezes blew just right, and she and her family sat on the porch and listened to her grandfather talk of his youth in days long past, when he sat upon the same porch and stared as Indians moved in the distance over the faraway hills. He talked of other things, forgotten now in the passage of time, but she remembers him sitting and staring at the star-filled sky. She painted a picture of an old man at rest with himself and the world, watching the pale moon glow.

The little girl that she once was talked of the clear night sky filled with stars that shimmered and shined, the moon hanging heavy in the western sky. She wrote of storms gathering, growing with awesome force in a darkening sky, and the crashing of thunder while she stood mute and watched with a little girl's wondering eyes. As I read her written words, I felt that I, too, was there. I could see the storm blowing in, feel the first chill winds tugging at my shoulders as the storm grew into a mighty thing, the rumble of the thunder as it announced its arrival with a ground-rattling boom. In my mind's eye, I stood beside her and her family and grandfather, too, and watched the wheeling stars in the pinpricked sky, felt the cool breath of the gentle evening's breeze.

She spoke of her parents, their lives and dreams, of her father returning from overseas at the end of the first World War in 1919, her parents' courtship and marriage, new branches growing on the old family tree. In time her parents took over the beloved family farm where she and her brother and sister grew up, their memories adding to its charm. One day she married and moved away, but the farm stayed in the family and still is today. She and her husband are now retired and live in a town. The home that she spoke of still sits by the side of the road, its old porch still beckoning to those who pass.

Many of the things she told of may come to pass in my life over time. Eventually my children will grow up, and maybe then my wife and I will retire and just sit on our porch and tell stories to our grandchildren of days gone by. I visited the old house that she spoke of, stood in its hall, and sat on the porch and thought of its memory-filled past. Like the porch of our old home, it has old-fashioned columns that were spun on a spinning lathe, and the paint clings to their curves in a halfhearted way, chalky and discolored with age, but the old porch is a comfortable place. It fits the soul and if you sit very still and listen, perhaps you can hear the squeak of her grandfather's chair as he sits and stares, recounting all the memories living there.

OPPOSITE: *The furnishings of a rural porch are secondary to the view. The beauty of the landscape surrounding Robert Frost's home must have provided inspiration for many of his poems.*

(The letter referred to in this story arrived a few days ago from a lady who had read a story that I wrote some time ago entitled "Porches." The letter was full of memories and I was delighted to receive it. I read it thoroughly and was so struck with its contents that I felt this short essay, which I have titled "Letter from the Porch," needed to be written and shared. —Richard R. Radtke)

CHAPTER TWO

Screened-In Spaces

The idea of the quintessential screened porch—all fitted out with wicker furniture wearing plump cushions, as well as with cozy afghans, rag rugs, and potted plants—conjures up an old-fashioned image. Yet it is actually a relatively recent innovation that probably did not make its debut until the end of the nineteenth or beginning of the twentieth century, when screening was widely available and applied to residential structures.

According to the Museum Services Center of the National Parks Service in Boston, the actual date when screening was first used in homes is not known, but the precedent to use the material may very well date to the practice that many eighteenth-century homeowners had of draping mosquito netting around their beds to protect themselves from unwanted pests. Screens probably came into existence in the mid-eighteenth century; one wire cloth mill in Clinton, Massachusetts, was known to produce window screening at that time. Using screening to keep pests out of homes, and eventually to keep pests off porches, was a natural progression. It was hastened still further by the architectural development of the Craftsman bungalow and its tremendous popularity in California, where it made sense to use porches all year long thanks to the clement weather.

The Craftsman style was a movement in architecture that developed in the eastern part of the United States, and the Craftsman bungalow emerged as one of its variations. The style's guiding force was the English Arts and Crafts movement, which was popularized in North America by Gustav Stickley in *The Craftsman*, the magazine he published from 1901 to 1916. The Craftsman style found its most sophisticated expression in the work of architects in California during the first quarter of the 1900s.

While the Craftsman style was translated into many types of homes—usually consisting of an exterior with rustic-looking building materials, deep overhangs with exposed rafter tails at the eaves, and a potpourri of pergolas and trellises over the porches—smaller bungalows were particularly prevalent. They were popularized by such magazines as *Ladies Home Journal*, which published designs for these smaller homes in their pages. Thus the Craftsman-style bungalow—typically a one-story cottage with a wide overhanging roof, a deep veranda at its front, and a porch or several porches tucked under the eaves or projecting overhangs—received widespread publicity. And the porches that graced these structures were often enclosed with screens, sometimes when the house was first built and other times as an afterthought.

OPPOSITE: *A log cabin's screened porch serves as many things: an entrance way, a reading spot, and a place to stash wet or dirty sporting gear. If it becomes necessary to turn this porch into an extra living space, more formal furniture and a rug can be added, some pictures hung from the walls, and the ceiling painted a cheerful hue.*

Though the Craftsman-style bungalows were probably the first homes to sport screened porches en masse in the United States, the "true" bungalow, with its more exotic pedigree, may have been the precursor to this practice. It was adapted from housing developed by British officers stationed in India in the 1890s (the period of the Raj), and its name stems from the word bangala, meaning "of Bengal." These houses had porches with wooden blinds and louvered shutters, which were most likely replaced with screening when the inexpensive, factory-produced version became widely available in the 1880s. These screens could be affixed permanently or removed when weather demanded, and worked far better than blinds or shutters.

In colder climates throughout the United States, screened porches were often associated with weekend and vacation homes, but they eventually came to grace year-round city and suburban homes. In the 1960s and 1970s, many homeowners lucky enough to have porches glassed in these spaces to gain more of a traditional living space. But those whose homes still have them or who have built new houses with screened porches know the joy of sitting or dining outdoors yet being protected from bugs and hot sun. And in many climates, such spaces can be used throughout the year.

Decorating Your Screened Porch

There's no right or wrong way to decorate your screened porch, but a casual look usually works best since this is a room that's partly outdoors and open to the weather—good and bad. Pick your seating carefully for comfort and wearability. Estate sales and flea markets often yield great buys on old wicker or wrought iron, which you won't have to worry about getting ruined in sudden downpours. If the porch is roomy enough, a cushy sofa can accommodate a lot of loungers. Easy chairs and rockers are also ideal seats to throw into the mix. For the adventurous, consider a two- or three-seat swing suspended from the ceiling as an alternative to the rocker, or a hammock instead of an easy chair or lounger.

Upholster pieces in a vinyl-covered material or other protected fabric, or a pretty chintz that has been treated with a stain inhibitor such as Scotchgard. Be sure that the coverings can be removed for easy cleaning

ABOVE: *Many bungalows such as this started their lives with front porches that were later screened in to gain a semi-protected living space as well as a more covered entryway. Either way, the porch provides a gracious entry and a nice place to sit and read the morning newspaper with a glass of fresh orange juice.*
OPPOSITE: *One of the perks of a screened porch is having a place to dine that's safe from hungry bugs yet doesn't forsake woodland views. In this lovely example, the owners placed plush towels across the backs of the rattan chairs for extra seating comfort and added two small pull-up benches for additional guests.*

at the end of the season. Avoid down fillers because of the room's potential dampness. Plan on including a dining table and chairs since dining alfresco is among the most pleasurable of spring, summer, and autumn rituals.

A buffet on wheels is an easy way to transport food from the kitchen to your porch. Also have on hand a large tray, which will come in handy for carrying dishes and food back and forth between the areas. Practical everyday dishes and cutlery are also better suited to this purpose than your fine china, crystal, and silver.

Plants thrive in a screened porch and are a great filler for corners where you may not have furniture. They also create a good visual link between the outdoors and indoors. Soft rag rugs add color and a comfortable surface for bare feet atop rigid wood floors. Although sisal matting looks attractive, it's not a good choice since it's hard to clean and will trap and hold pollen and food.

Don't forget to have on hand enough lighting and some citronella candles for those itty-bitty bugs that are able to get through the smallest mesh screening.

Adding a Ceiling Fan

The purpose of a ceiling fan has not changed much since its debut. It still helps keep a room or porch cool and breezy on a hot day. But the way it looks and how it functions have changed dramatically from the days when Humphrey Bogart uttered the famous words "Play it, Sam." Today you have many more styles and types of fans to consider.

First, the fans appropriate for use on a screened porch or an outdoor terrace are different from the ones used in interiors, because the housing and blades must be wired for outdoor use and protected so that they do not short out when it rains or snows.

LEFT: *Screened porches can be quite dressy when furniture is upholstered in fancy checks and florals, and the dining table is set with good china and cutlery. Lamps, flowers, and a ceiling fan give this one all the comforts of indoor living.*

OPPOSITE: *A patio flanked by a screened porch has year-round appeal. This porch is furnished with wicker pieces that are comfortable and give the room an airy feeling all year long, even when the sliding doors are shut because of inclement winter weather.* ABOVE: *A study or den can take on a porchlike appearance with rustic furnishings. The next step in this cozy home would be to add sliding doors that provide access to the outdoors.*

TIPS ON BUILDING AND UPKEEP

If you add a new screened porch, be sure you orient it in the direction that suits your preferences best—toward or away from the sun and toward the best views, your garden, and cooling breezes. If your porch is already built and receiving too much sun, consider adding overhangs or awnings for extra protection.

~ Have a weather-resistant solid floor, since rain and snow will come through. Consider having some type of mesh wire beneath the floorboards to make it harder for insects and bugs to crawl through. The best choices for flooring are ceramic tile and slate. The worst choices are wood and carpeting, which get wet and develop mildew.

~ Be sure the bottom of your screening near the floor has some space for the rainwater to run off or the frame, if wood, will rot.

~ Use aluminum frames rather than wood to house the screening since they don't decay and won't need to be replaced.

~ Install a skylight (if you don't have a room above your porch) so that you can see the sky, sun, and stars and get more light.

~ If you want to extend the use of your porch, insulate the walls and ceilings with fiberglass batting, install thermopane windows with screens that offer insulation, or use screening that, come autumn and winter, you can completely remove and replace with glass panes (called an interchangeable storm and screen). Your room will work for three seasons of the year; add some form of heat and you'll achieve a four-season room.

~ If your screening develops a hole or a rip, you can patch it yourself with a needle and heavy-duty thread, though it won't look terribly professional. Or you can have that single frame rewired.

~ Screens require almost no maintenance—only an occasional cleaning with soap and a scrub brush. Screened porches can potentially get filthy with pollen and dust, which you can clean off with a large paintbrush. Be prepared to vacuum the porch well.

~ How long screens last depends on what materials are used. The uncoated aluminum screens found on older homes are often oxidized and pitted, which is equivalent to rust.

Eventually, when this screening is eaten away, it must be replaced. Today you can buy coated aluminum that continues to look good over a long period and doesn't decay. You can also buy fiberglass mesh, which is much cheaper than coated aluminum, but it often stretches out over time and looks bad.

~ Though some manufacturers may advertise standard-size screens, these are rarely available and you'll most likely end up purchasing custom screens.

OPPOSITE: *Though a beach cottage is the obvious structure to sport a screened porch, putting one on a primary residence gives the home added flexibility. The space can be used—as weather allows—to call to mind the relaxing atmosphere of the beach and set a casual tone at home. Further emphasizing the beach house ambience is the fact that this wraparound porch is the perfect place to sleep on warm summer nights, safe from biting insects and open to fresh, cool breezes.*

ABOVE: *A screened porch can be built to face a lush garden, to offer homeowners the feeling of really getting away. The glass-topped café table, slat chairs, and ceiling fan contribute to the vacation feeling. Be conscious of fragrances when planning the garden— the more varied scents the better.*

OPPOSITE: *This simple screened porch is small on space but big on comfort. The wicker chair and love seat are made comfortable with plump cushions and a cheery assortment of throw pillows. A tiny antique trunk and a tape-seat stool make unique and attractive tables.*

Once you choose a proper functional design, be sure it fits with the look of your space. Many options now exist, from classic Victorian fans with lots of ornate trim on the housing and with old-fashioned-style wooden blades to sleek, spare, contemporary fans in glossy blacks, whites, and reds. Most ceiling fans come with five blades; some, however, require you to purchase the blades separately.

You'll need to decide whether you want the fan to function as a light as well. If so, you need to buy a light kit that attaches to the housing. Buy the brightest bulbs you can, since the area probably won't be illuminated from other sources, though some people prefer to use pink bulbs for a soft, romantic light. Some ceiling fans, however, already feature a lighting fixture in their design.

If the ceiling is very high, you'll also need to buy a down rod or pole so that the fan will hang lower. Measure the height of the room before you go shopping for your fan.

Finally, decide whether you are happy jumping up and down and pulling a cord to turn on the fan and light or whether you prefer to do your switching from the comfort of a chair or sofa. If so, you'll want to buy a remote switch systems which controls your fan in the same way that you can control your television set.

WICKER FURNITURE

Ralph Lauren may have helped to make wicker furnishings fashionable once again by re-creating the ambience of long-ago summer porches filled with wicker settees, armchairs, and tables that have fanciful curlicues and dense latticework, but the history of wicker goes back much further. Wicker is a broad term for furniture woven from willow, reed, cane, raffia, fiber-rush (twisted paper), sea grass, and other materials; the word comes from the Scandinavian *vika*, which means "to bend."

A statue of an official sitting on a reed hassock was found in Mesopotamia in 2600 B.C., according to Richard Saunders, author of *Wicker Furniture: A Guide to Restoring & Collecting* (Crown Publishers). A reed wig box was found in Egypt in 1400 B.C. The Romans and Greeks used wicker furniture as well.

In the United States, wicker became popular after Massachusetts grocer Cyrus Wakefield created an entrepreneurial niche for himself. In the 1840s he noticed that ships returning to Boston from China discarded the reeds they used to protect their cargo. Wakefield recycled the material into furniture,

which was originally used indoors. He founded the Wakefield Rattan Co. in the town of South Reading, Massachusetts, which was later renamed Wakefield in his honor. At Wakefield Rattan, workers made dozens of wicker furnishings by hand, including buffets, posing chairs for photographers' models, baby carriages, rockers, and tête-à-tête seats to enable lovebirds to sit close—but not too close.

After Wakefield died in 1873, heirs merged the firm with its main competitor, Heywood Brothers and Co., and the new company,

Heywood Brothers and Wakefield Co.—later shortened to Heywood-Wakefield—opened other factories nationwide, including one in Chicago. Wicker furnishings changed with the invention of the Lloyd loom in 1917, which allowed weavers to construct wicker faster. Heywood-Wakefield purchased the patented loom in 1920. As the economy slowed and manufacturers turned out inferior-quality wicker at lower prices, the material began to lose its appeal. Heywood-Wakefield stopped making wicker in the 1930s, although the firm produced hardwood furniture into the 1950s.

In the late 1800s, as people fled to the country in search of fresh air, homeowners moved their wicker outdoors to their porches. Wicker was considered a healthy material for furnishings since it was believed that fresh air could blow germs away from it. Through the decades, wicker furnishings reflected changing design styles. Victorian wicker, in its heyday from 1880 to 1910, was fanciful in its forms, imitating hearts, peacocks, and cornucopias. Distinct styles existed such as Cape Cod, which wove fibers tightly together, and Bar Harbor, which featured open lattice-work. The Arts and Crafts wicker furniture that followed was more rectilinear, and Art Deco wicker emerged in the 1920s.

Choosing the best wicker requires care and diligence. Because the finest examples of antique wicker were made on a hardwood frame, they are sturdier than many pieces made today, which are built over hollow bamboo frames. Do not choose anything with a frame that is broken. Another sign of good wicker is curlicues that are tightly wound. While a natural-color finish may reflect age, that is not always the case since much old wicker was painted, lacquered, and stained over the years, hiding its original coloration. Many old pieces have retained their original labels, with the paper stickers glued underneath the seats or other parts of the design.

Collectors should also try to avoid pieces with too little weaving, since these won't hold their value or structure. These were made at a

OPPOSITE: *Wicker has been used to craft furniture in myriad styles. Looks for pieces with tightly woven reeds over sturdy frames, such as the furnishings in this reproduction Victorian ensemble. A wicker birdcage on a stand completes the period look.* ABOVE: *There is nothing fresher or more evocative of an airy outside setting than white wicker. If you plan on using wicker outside, make sure that the pieces have been treated so all parts (including cushions) are weatherproof.*

time when many factories began skimping on workmanship and leaving off arm supports and other details. Also avoid pieces whose proportions are too top- or bottom-heavy, and stay away from items that have been heavily painted, since these can be hard to strip. Finally, avoid those that have a hairy look and feel, because they were constructed of reeds that frayed and will not hold up over time.

Quality antique wicker continues to appreciate in value, though dealers disagree

on how much. Prices tend to be higher on the East Coast and particularly so for sets with a number of matched pieces. Auctions, estate sales, and antique shops are all good hunting grounds. Publications such as *Maine Antique Digest,* published in Waldoboro, Maine, feature advertisements. Another good source for further reading is Jeremy Adamson's *American Wicker.*

CHAPTER THREE

All Glassed In

*I*nclement weather sometimes makes it impossible to enjoy the great outdoors, but glassed-in rooms, such as sunrooms and conservatories, allow us to bring the outside in all year long. Whether it's been glazed just to allow you to enjoy the bright light of the sun or to take advantage of a spectacular view, such spaces offer great bonuses to many homeowners. Some can be used year-round, depending on how they're constructed or where they are located, but all offer protection from the elements and from pesky bugs. Such attributes are decidedly an asset for a wide range of activities, especially entertaining and eating.

The earliest example of a glass room probably dates to 1543 in Pisa, Italy; it was used for raising plants. One of the first well-known glassed-in spaces was the royal greenhouse built by Sir Christopher Wren at Hampton Court Palace in England in the late sixteenth century. Greenhouses became popular throughout England and France as places to shelter and raise orange, lemon, and lime trees when the weather turned cold.

New technological breakthroughs—the abilities to produce larger sheets of glass, make the framing to house the glass more flexible, and improve heating through the use of hot water—led to impressive glass constructions such as Sir Joseph Paxton's famous iron and glass Crystal Palace, which was built in London for the Great Exhibition of 1851. In fact, the late nineteenth century was the golden era of conservatories, when they were built as places to raise other living forms of greenery besides fruit trees.

The transition from utilizing a glassed room for a greenhouse to using it as a place solely for people was only a matter of time. By the latter part of the Victorian era, people had grown tired of dark, dimly lit rooms. At the same time, they were concerned about health issues because of the polluted air in cities, and they sought healthy environments to escape communicable diseases such as tuberculosis, which was relatively widespread at the time. Thomas Edison was known to have a glass room in his New Jersey home: photographs show the Edison family sitting in the room.

The popularity of the glassed-in room swelled in the 1950s, when numerous suburban families enclosed their open or screened porches to gain more living space, particularly after the invention of the television had driven families to congregate indoors. Even city apartment dwellers enclose balconies of all sizes to gain extra year-round square footage.

OPPOSITE: *The tiny side porch of this old stone house was glassed in so that the owners would have a sunny place to enjoy their morning coffee year-round. Creature comforts include a colorful array of kilim pillows, plenty of greenery and flowers, and good natural light to read by.*

Today many homeowners have chosen to add modern versions of old-fashioned conservatories that are constructed of aluminum, timber, or vinyl and glass. Many of these conservatories come in kits that can be assembled by do-it-yourselfers or by professional carpenters or builders, and in many cases they can be attached to almost any room of a house.

Price and function will determine the size of your conservatory. As a living space, a two-hundred-square-foot (18.5 sq m) conservatory—about ten by twenty feet (3 by 6m)—is quite typical. Once built, the conservatory often becomes the focal point of a house, since it is exceedingly light, airy, and well insulated. All conservatories offer solar access, which can be further controlled through window shades or tinted glass, depending on the room's orientation. Any greenhouse room should be built with a full foundation.

The most aesthetically and functionally successful glassed rooms don't pretend to be what they're not—formal spaces—and instead are furnished a bit differently than other communal areas in a home, such as living rooms and dens. Part of the reason is that glassed rooms have traditionally been damper. Good antiques, expensive fabrics, important Oriental carpets, and prized artwork simply do not hold up to the increased humidity of a glassed-in space.

But such a room also offers homeowners a much-needed outlet for a bit of playful creativity—a space where they can kick up their feet. Fanciful architecture such as latticework trim, exuberant arches, columns, and beaded ceilings look great mixed and matched in these glass havens. Brighter palettes also look perkier when the sun shines through these rooms' glass reaches, and on gray days having the outdoors peek through helps awaken the entire house and its occupants. Finally, more casual furnishings and accessories work best in these rooms since they are less likely to be damaged. And the possibilities are extensive, from wicker tables and chairs to wooden rocking chairs, swings, hammocks, and big pots or urns of greenery and fresh flowers.

OPPOSITE: Polished wood floors, leaded glass windows, a floral ottoman used as a table, and large potted plants add Victorian elegance to an enclosed front porch. The Mission-style rocking chairs make it a bit rustic and cozy and illustrate that no room has to be furnished completely in one style.

ABOVE: A glassed-in porch can be dressed up with a floor of black and white tiles set on a diagonal rather than a traditional stone or brick treatment. Shades overhead can be opened and closed depending on the amount of sunlight; a ceiling fan helps keep the people and plants cool and at their prime. The overall charm of the room comes from its graceful yet comfortable decor.

COLOR

White may be a perennial favorite for porches because it connotes old-fashioned summer goodness, and you may decide to make your porch, deck, sunroom, or gazebo all white. But don't feel constrained. With a blue sky, green grass, and a garden full of flower and herb colors surrounding you in summer—and perhaps the rest of the year, depending on your locale—there's no reason you can't use any favorite shade as your primary choice for the porch, or as an accent color.

Other than your garden, where else can you find inspiration? Maybe from your wardrobe, work environment, favorite foods, or a cherished piece of furniture or art. Thinking of color as a mood enhancer may also be a good way to get started. Because of their typically

LEFT: *Porch furniture is perfect for injecting color into a space, especially if the pieces are old and can be given a new coat of paint. Here, the cool hues used on the furnishings coordinate with those of the shutters, which were hung strictly for their decorative prowess. The bright table setting and myriad flowers add warmth to what might otherwise be a somber color scheme.* OPPOSITE: *Color can go a long way in enhancing the charm of a space, as this tiny porch shows. It has been dressed up with a simple but highly effective coordinating color scheme.*

casual mood, porches are a good place to get a bit playful, if not downright zany, in a way that you might feel uncomfortable doing in your more formal living or dining room. Consider painting the ceiling or floor of your porch or other outdoor space in one or two hues that are different than the color of the rest of the structure, or even in stripes, clouds, or polka dots. Remember to use a paint and sealer that will withstand rain and wind.

Porch furniture is also a good place to inject color, particularly if the furniture is old and needs a fresh coat of paint. You could consider painting each of those old family rocking chairs you inherited in a different color so that you have the entire crayon box represented in a rainbow of seats, which can then be placed all in a row.

You can also add color a bit less permanently (though paint is certainly easy to use and inexpensive to change) through your choice of cushions, pillows, or awnings—or even in the much smaller decorating accessory choices such as watering cans, table place mats, plastic drink tumblers, and vases.

But don't forget one of color's main benefits. It can work architectural magic. If you want a high-ceilinged porch to appear lower and cozier, paint it a darker color. And if you choose to go with white, make smart choices by using fabrics, paints, and rugs that are washable. Porches are one place you should always be able to take off your shoes and put your feet up without raising any eyebrows.

LEFT: *Kilims, pillows, and upholstery in a variety of bright colors and patterns create a space worthy of a palace in* The Arabian Nights. *Pots of red amaryllis and a tray of fresh-picked lemons accentuate the hues of the textiles. Built-in stone benches covered with plump cushions, a collection of urns both great and small, and a hanging iron candelabra add to the exotic flavor.* OPPOSITE: *When the guest list increases, the owners of this traditional home often set another table in their trellis- and glass-walled porch, furnished with antiques and reproduction furnishings. Sometimes they also use this space for family meals, preferring the more casual tone of the room to their antique-filled dining room.*

Types of Windows

There are many window options for enclosed porches, ranging from simple glass rectangles or squares to those that incorporate the flourish of a circle head window. Different shapes, styles, and sizes can be combined to form myriad configurations and can greatly alter the appearance of a porch and how it relates to the design of its home. But you need to choose carefully—remember that all windows are long-term investments that should be as suitable to the structure in twenty-five years as when they were first installed.

Following is a list of the main types of windows that can be used when building a porch.

AWNING WINDOW. With one or more hinged sashes at the top, this window tilts outward and usually has a low-maintenance exterior in aluminum with a baked-enamel finish. It opens and closes with a cranking system of some sort, is easy to clean, offers good ventilation, and can be used in combination with casement windows.

BAY WINDOW. This type of window features a large fixed center panel flanked by vent units that have operable sashes joining the wall of the structure. The side panels jut out at a 45-degree angle. A bay window can be a full-height configuration or have a window seat incorporated into its design.

BOW WINDOW. Similar to a bay window, this vent-size unit has sides that are curved instead of extending straight from the angle. Like a bay window, it lends a spacious look and architectural cachet to a structure.

CASEMENT WINDOW. This swings open from one side thanks to the sash openings on hinges that are attached to the upright side of the frame. It usually has levers or cranking systems to open and close it and can be found framed in wood or with a low-maintenance exterior of aluminum with a baked-enamel finish. It is usually part of a series of similarly sized windows, which are often subdivided by muntins. Some newer versions offer casements as part of a whole metal window unit that includes windows that do not open and are topped by a transom.

CIRCLE HEAD WINDOW. Used in combination with casement and/or double-hung windows or doors, circle head windows are available in different circular or elliptical shapes, as well as arched or cathedral configurations, both with and without muntins. They can be found with low-maintenance aluminum exteriors and in many special sizes and configurations.

ABOVE: *More a room addition than a glassed-in porch, this space has large Palladian-style windows that are left bare to enjoy views of the backyard. The orientation of the room makes a window treatment unnecessary, since the indirect light is gentle on the furnishings and occupants.* OPPOSITE: *Three walls of this tiny side porch were fitted with casement windows to create a cozy sitting room that also serves as a playroom for visiting children. The over-stuffed sofa and armchair provide the only spots of color in an all-white space, but their cheery yellow and lime green are the perfect accents for this room surrounded by foliage and sunlight.*

~ *DOUBLE-HUNG WINDOW.* Two vertically sliding sashes, one above the other and each closing a different part of the window, give this type of window its name. One or both slide up and down; the frames may be of equal size, or one may be larger than the other. The frames are often subdivided with muntins and are usually constructed of wood, but low-maintenance exteriors are available in aluminum with baked-enamel finishes. In newer windows, the sash can also slide horizontally.

~ *FANLIGHT.* Used over another window or even over a door, this window has a semicircular or elliptical shape.

~ *FIXED-GLASS WINDOW.* As the name implies, this window doesn't open. Fixed-glass windows come in a variety of shapes and are generally used in conjunction with other types of windows that are operable.

~ *HOPPER WINDOW.* Much the same as a casement window, this has a sash hinged at the bottom instead of at the top and is primarily used for below-grade construction.

~ *PICTURE WINDOW.* A very large window uninterrupted by mullions, this window is often fixed and cannot be opened; it is typically placed to provide an attractive vista.

~ *SIDELIGHT.* A window located at the side of a door or another window; it is also called a winglight.

~ *TRANSOM.* A hinged window over another window or door, this swings open but is hinged at the top.

WINDOW HARDWARE

Several different types of hardware must be considered when installing a window.

~ *CASEMENT FASTENERS.* Two fittings are necessary for a casement—a fastener at the side and a stay along the bottom that keeps the window closed or allows it to be left open without flapping. Some metal casements have a cockspur fastener, wherein the part that turns back to the window has a few grooves that allow the window to be opened just a crack for ventilation.

~ *ESPAGNOLETTE.* This long vertical bolt is installed on the inside edges of a pair of French doors. A handle fitted on one side turns the bolt, which shoots up and down into the window frame.

~ *SASH FASTENERS.* Fitted into window frames, these devices secure the two parts of a double-hung window, pushing them apart vertically and together horizontally. They should be inserted firmly into a window frame to reduce drafts. They come in a variety of designs but are most often made of iron, which needs to be oiled or painted, or lacquered brass, which requires no treatment.

WINDOW WISDOM

indows, which come in myriad shapes and sizes, are naturally the most important components of a glassed-in room. Whether the porch is completely constructed of glass or just features wide stretches of glass, it will incorporate large amounts of the material in the form of various types of windows.

Unlike many other building components, windows already come in standard shapes, styles, and sizes, making them much more than a mere material. They are, in effect, architectural embellishments and must relate to the period, style, and decor of a home. Consequently, when adding a porch that is either glassed-in or filled with many windows, it is critical to be sensitive

to the rest of the structure. Of course, you can have windows custom-made, but that is an expensive proposition.

Multipaned Georgian-style sash windows may be out of place on a mid-century bungalow, while expansive sheet glass windows will be totally wrong on a frothy Victorian. The windows should look as if they were always there. When building or adding a glassed-in room, match or coordinate with the pane size and proportions of the windows that already exist on the structure. For instance, in a historic residence with mullioned windows, a glassed-in porch should incorporate the same type of window. Though there is no obligation to continue the tradition, ignoring it can create a structural disparity, diminish the value of the entire home, and anger neighbors who have to look at an unsightly addition.

LEFT: Elegant twin English-style conservatories have been added to this house to serve as living and dining rooms with a spectacular view. Even the ceilings are glazed to make the most of the sunlight.
OPPOSITE: This octagonal porch is enclosed with leaded, arched, Gothic-style windows that are in keeping with the original structure. The wide doors also have a graceful arch at the top, and a border pattern of stenciling and a collection of fine china on the wall add to the nineteenth-century ambience.

ABOVE: *What do you do with an extensive collection of quilts and blankets when you don't have an attic or a waterproof basement? Stack them in an attractive cupboard and leave the doors permanently ajar to display them. Add some willow chairs and you've created a charming rustic scene.*

OPPOSITE: *The Arts and Crafts–style wood and glass design lends itself to a glassed-in porch, particularly when the panes run floor to ceiling with decorative inserts and the floor is paved in a similar wood. The owners have left the furnishings minimal so that they can use the room for dance parties or set up extra tables for dining.*

Decorative Window Treatments

The purpose of a glassed-in room is to conjure up the great outdoors. These are not spaces meant for formal accoutrements, although with the proper structural enhancements they can certainly accommodate fine furnishings and be fitted formally. But most homeowners who create glassed-in spaces want them to have the ambience of an open porch.

There will probably be more glass than any other material in many of these spaces, although some glassed-in rooms have a few solid walls. If there are actually more solid walls than glass walls, or if you want to create the effect of a glassed-in room, opt for minimal window treatments to bring the outdoors in. Regardless of how many windows a space has, some sort of window treatment may be necessary since drapes, curtains, blinds, shutters, and shades help regulate heat, reduce noise, and ensure privacy. Following is information on a variety of decorative treatments that can be used to turn a space into one that resembles the "great indoors."

CURTAINS AND DRAPES

Curtains and drapes can be crafted of virtually any material, from burlap to silk, although they may be difficult to use in a glassed-in room. It may not be possible to affix the appropriate hardware to the windows in the room, or there may be whole walls of glass that will be difficult to treat in this manner. There are dozens of types of drapes or curtains to choose from, and they can be custom-made by professionals or home-sewn. Regardless of style, type, or fabric chosen for this sort of treatment, there are a few general pointers to keep in mind.

~ The architecture of the room should influence the choice of fabric. For informal rooms, materials that have a casual flair and are normally used for clothing—such as ticking, shirting, or madras—can often be crafted into appropriate and stunning window treatments.

~ Drapes and curtains will last a lot longer if the dust is removed from them frequently. Dirt that builds up on the fabric is broken down by the sun. To clean, vacuum or shake them out on a regular basis.

~ A lining gives extra weight and body to curtains and drapes, conceals all hems and raw edges, and, most importantly, protects the fabric from light and prolongs the life of the window treatment.

OPPOSITE: *Decorative treatments such as blinds and drapes can enhance a space by reducing noise, regulating sunlight and temperature, ensuring privacy, and even modifying awkward proportions. Here, a series of swags in a simple checked fabric lends intimacy and warmth to an oversized space.* ABOVE: *Like a giant skylight, the roof of an addition was totally glazed to bring in plenty of sunlight, blue sky, and stars at night. All the fabrics were found at a remnant sale to cut down on upholstery costs.*

~ While the fabric conveys ambience and effect, the heading (the gathering or pleating at the top) actually defines the style of a curtain or drape. French pleats are small clusters of three pleats grouped at regular intervals; pencil pleats are tighter and run continuously across the curtain (they work particularly well with lightweight or sheer fabrics); gathered headings are a cross between French and pencil pleats; and cartridge pleats are elaborate and more formal, with stiff cuffs that are stuffed with interlining.

~ Curtains and drapes are secured at the top with either poles and finials or rods. Poles and finials are visual elements that are meant to be visible, and consequently they are available in many decorative versions today. Poles can be made of traditional materials such as brass, steel, or wood, though they also come in creative variations such as wrought iron or driftwood. Finials, the decorative caps that end the poles, are made in myriad shapes and sizes, ranging from simple and spare to ornate and flamboyant. Rods, on the other hand, are normally hidden behind the curtain headings. They are available in many sizes and can be custom-made to fit the awkwardly shaped windows that are often prevalent in glassed-in rooms.

~ Cornices and valances are more formal treatments that need to be positioned at the top of the window over curtain or drape headings. While cornices are generally formed over a wood base, valances are made entirely from cloth.

~ Tiebacks manipulate curtains or drapes into graceful folds when they are drawn back, but are also structurally functional since they alleviate the stress that the weight of the curtain or drape puts on its pole or rod. They can be fashioned from almost anything, from fabric to cording to metal chains, and can be used as an unusual decorative enhancement.

BLINDS, SHUTTERS, AND SHADES

With their clean, straightforward lines, these treatments are much simpler and less dramatic than curtains and drapes. They are also extremely practical and always appropriate, especially in a glassed-in room. For large windows, which will very likely be present in these spaces, it is more practical and attractive to hang several separate shades instead of a single shade across the horizontal expanse of the whole window. This also allows greater flexibility in controlling the shade and light in the room.

Though these treatments come in hundreds of incarnations, the following are the most popular and easy to adapt to a glassed-in room.

Roller shades, which simply pull down, are the all-time classic and come in a wide range of ready-made sizes or can be custom-made. They are suitable alone, especially in specialty fabrics, but are often used as undertreatments for curtains or drapes. Though they can be made of virtually any material and now come in such creative materials as taffeta and metallic meshes, tight, flat weaves work best. Loose weaves will roll unevenly or wear out quickly, so take these points into consideration when having custom shades made. Honeycomb shades let sunlight flood the space during the day but help insulate the room at night.

OPPOSITE: *This elegant sunroom has a unique design: a series of French doors has been used instead of fixed windows. Roman shades in a subtle striped pattern can be pulled down when the sun is too bright for comfort.*

INSULATED GLASS

To make a glass room work most effectively, you must choose your glass carefully, especially since about 15 percent of the heat a home loses escapes through the windows. Fortunately, many new options are available today, though some are more cost-effective than others. Some may also affect the architectural integrity of your home (modern double- or triple-glazed windows don't look right on a historic structure, for example), so do your best to match the frames to those of the home's existing windows.

Clear insulating glass offers you heat gain and, at the same time, a high R-value (the term for the amount of insulation provided). New glazing, called high-performance glass or low-E glass, provides a much higher R-value than normal clear insulating glass, but blocks the sun's rays. Low-E glass is the optimum in high performance in both winter and summer, making it more effective year-round than passive

solutions that work only in the cold. It filters a high percentage of the sun's ultraviolet rays, which fade interior fabrics and furnishings. Other advantages are that it's clear, low-cost, and proven to work.

Double-glazed windows minimize condensation and the cold zone that occurs around windows in a room, while triple glazing offers even greater insulating values, making the space more comfortable in extremely hot or cold weather. The downside to triple glazing is the lower light transmission and poorer glass clarity that occur because you are looking through three pieces of glass.

If you want to create a solar-heated glass room, try to orient your room in a southern direction. Install some window coverings to deflect excess light, add a fan to counter heat buildup during warmer months and move the air around, and use tile, stone, brick, or any other masonry material on the floor to retain the heat.

LEFT: *Thanks to all the types of glass now available, a skylight doesn't have to be halfhearted. This one goes from skylight to full-blown roof and helps transform this great room into a year-round "open-air" room. A bank of arched Gothic-style windows provides a second entrance for precious sunlight.* OPPOSITE: *Because the summer season is short on the coast of Maine, the owners of a large, old cottage glassed in their porch for more living space and better views of the craggy shoreline beyond. But as in other colder climates, the room becomes the most used space as soon as the sun shines. Afghans and blankets provide warmth on chilly evenings.*

Roman shades work on a simple cording system that draws the shade up into a series of broad, flat folds. They are attached to dowel rods, which secure them horizontally and are concealed in a pocket made from the fabric. When unrolled, Roman shades resemble ordinary blinds, but they take on a much more dramatic demeanor when pulled up to half-mast. Although plainer fabrics can look rather bland unrolled, large patterns will be distorted and look awkward when they are pulled up, so keep this in mind when choosing fabric. Stripes are a good choice for Roman shades. Lining these shades improves the way the pleats fall and blocks out more light.

Austrian shades and *balloon shades* combine the graceful, draped effect of curtains with the operative workings of a Roman shade. They are ruched and gathered—Austrian shades end in deep ruched scallops; balloon shades are ruched from top to bottom and gathered from side to side. When pulled up with cords that run the length of the shades through a looped tape at the back, these types of curtains achieve a ballooned effect that looks quite ornate. Plain fabrics or simple stripes are best for these fancy forms, since large-scale patterns generally look too busy.

Venetian blinds are usually made of two-inch (5cm) slats; in small widths they are called mini blinds or micro minis. They are available in a variety of materials, including fabric, vinyl, aluminum, and wood, and come in many colors, patterns, and finishes. They can be made to fit virtually any window, including those with unusual or odd shapes. They offer superb light control because they pivot open or closed, can be lowered or raised, and can also be motorized and operated by remote control. Blinds fabricated out of vinyl are less likely to twist or bow over time.

Shutters, which are mounted on each side of a window, are a crisp treatment that lends definition and polish. However, they are not suitable for whole walls of glass since they need a bit of wall space for mounting purposes. Most are made of wood and are louvered to let in fresh air and to filter or direct light. Old shutters can be recycled by trimming and repainting them to fit new windows.

WINDOW TRICKS

Windows can be beautiful as well as functional, and you can use them in a variety of ways to add architectural interest and decorative magic to your home.

~ Tiny windows appear bigger if their frames are painted white.

~ If you'd like to play down the size of a very large window, opt for mullions. These strips are a sort of grid system that become a part of the structure of the glass and cut the window visually into several smaller sections or many smaller panes. They work best on windows with at least three feet (91.5cm) of uninterrupted glass.

~ Glass blocks allow light to pass through but aren't transparent, so they can be used to create areas that are still suffused with light but seem more private.

OPPOSITE: *No other color suggests outdoors and summer as much as white does, used here for the tablecloth, banquette upholstery, and the billowy window shades. The banquette can double as a daybed for naps on sunny afternoons.*

ABOVE: *This glassed-in room has been transformed into a dressy new dining room, thanks to the balloon shades and fabric tenting at the ceiling, graceful furniture, a few choice pieces of silver, and even a chandelier. Besides gaining a larger eating space, the owners now have a room with great daytime views that they can use for lunch and weekend brunch.* OPPOSITE: *In this period English house, fabric is draped beneath the conservatory's glass roof to keep sunlight from making the room too hot, fading the furniture, and drying out the plants. The lovely Gothic windows, high-backed couch, French armchair, and Oriental rug add to the elegance of this room.*

RIGHT: *This gracious conservatory becomes a year-round living space with attractive cane, wicker, and wrought-iron furniture and elegant topiaries. A classically inspired marble and glass table serves up a light lunch and cool beverages.*
OPPOSITE: *This elegant space is furnished with a glass-topped table and decorative wire chairs to allow the owners to enjoy "alfresco" meals. The brick floor adds to the feeling of being in an outdoor café.*

To veil a window without losing light, add a layer of translucent glass on the lower half of the window, leaving the top half transparent. Translucent glass comes in a variety of styles, such as ribbed, leaded, or beveled.

If the windows in your sunroom face south, the heat and glare from the sun can be overwhelming in the afternoon, fading furniture and artwork and forcing you to crank up the air conditioning, which increases energy bills. Reduce sunlight without compromising the view with window shades made of Mylar, a dark, see-through plastic film that is equivalent to putting sunglasses on the room. Shade suppliers make these to order.

Dark fabrics on lighter window frames make a window's silhouette more sculptural by graphically delineating its outline.

HEATING A GLASS ROOM

What type of heat you add depends on your existing heating system. If you have hot-water heat, you
can run a circuit over to your glass room. If you're
willing to do a bit more remodeling of the room
and the floor—and you don't mind spending a bit
more—you can install an in-floor heating element,
which will warm the room and make the floor nice
and toasty. If you have a forced-air system and
your existing equipment is large enough, you can
run a trunk line in to heat the room. The downside
to this is that the thermostat will be in a different
part of the house, which will make it more of a
procedure to change the heat, and you're likely to
feel temperature swings. You can also install a self-
contained wall unit with a forced-air system. All
these options cost several thousand dollars for an
average ten- by twenty-foot (3 by 6m) room, but
the resulting benefit of increased use of the room
may be worth it.

Floor Treatments

A variety of floor coverings can be used in
glassed-in rooms. Concrete, brick, tile, flagstone,
wood, vinyl, rubber, linoleum, and cork (all dis-
cussed in chapter one) can work just as well
indoors as out. But a number of natural materials
are also ideal candidates for the glassed-in room,
including sisal, rush, sea grass, and coir.

Sisal, a hard fiber that is thicker and stiffer
than jute, flax, or hemp, is woven to make carpets
or mats in many shapes and sizes. Nowadays it has
been elevated to designer status, and is given a
wide range of decorative embellishments with dye

and paint that completely change its character from simple to grand. Sisal matting also comes in a variety of attractive woven patterns, which can add a subtler design element to a glassed-in room. It's antistatic, relatively easy to keep clean, hard-wearing, and versatile, especially since it can be dressed up or down. It comes with latex or cotton backing, and can be laid wall-to-wall like fabric carpeting or made into area rugs, mats, or runners. It must be cared for like carpeting, so it must be vacuumed, and it can be treated with Scotchgard. Spills should be blotted with absorbent paper immediately, and small knots should be trimmed with scissors (take care not to sever an important yarn that holds the weave).

Rush is a long grass that can be twisted and woven into mats but is best known for its use as the material forming the seats of provincial chairs. When it is used as a floor covering, hand-plaited strips are usually sewn together to fit the entire room or hall. Because it is not backed with any material, care must be taken when moving furniture on it (wheels and legs get caught), and it is not appropriate for stairs. It is usually laid loosely, even when it is used as a wall-to-wall carpet (it can be padded underneath in this context). It must be periodically lifted and dusted, and should be doused with water at least once a week to prevent tears, cracks, and flaking.

Sea grass is a hard, almost impermeable fiber grown in paddy fields. It is spun into tough strands and woven into practical flooring. It is softer and smoother underfoot and more resistant to stains than its other natural cousins, but it can't be given the wide range of decorative treatments that sisal can withstand. It can be fitted wall-to-wall or used as area carpeting, and should be vacuumed regularly. Use a stain-inhibiting treatment on it, and for severe dirt and mud stains, use a stiff brush along the grain once the stain has dried, then vacuum it.

Coir is the fiber from the husk of a coconut that in the past was used chiefly in making rope or matting. Today it is crafted into stylish carpets since it is sturdy and easier to keep clean than sisal, but it is also more expensive. It is now available in mats, area rugs, tiles, and wall-to-wall strips that are stitched together, and it can be backed with latex to prevent dust penetration and to increase its durability. It's ideal for high-traffic areas, and should be given a stain-inhibiting treatment and vacuumed regularly. It can become moldy in damp or humid conditions; if this happens, it should be brushed immediately.

ABOVE: *A semicircular porch is given a slightly exotic cast with a stone mosaic floor, jeweled stained glass windows, and blue and white furnishings that are pushed to the center of the room for a cozier feeling.*

OPPOSITE: *To take maximum advantage of growing space, the owners of this conservatory hang plants in baskets from the ceiling, place some on tables, and put the largest on the tiled floor, which is impervious to watering overflows. Tile is an ideal flooring material for greenhouses and conservatories for this reason, and earthy colors such as terra-cotta and black add to the natural charm of the space.*

Wall Treatments

Regardless of how much glass your glassed-in room may have, there's always a wall or two to account for (unless you're working with a conservatory). The way you address those walls can set the mood, establish the durability, affect the physical atmosphere, and influence the spatial dimensions of the room. Wood paneling or brick, for instance, can make a space seem rustic, while sisal or coir matting can give walls a textured, contemporary personality. The paneling or brick will be far more durable, but sisal and coir have thermal qualities that will insulate the room. They can also make the room seem more spacious.

Here are some pointers on three types of wall treatments that are popular in glassed-in rooms.

Vinyl and synthetic wall coverings are ideal in glassed-in rooms because they project an informal ambience and because they are durable and scrubbable; come in many colors, textures, and patterns; and can be used to solve a variety of design problems. If a wall is riddled with surface imperfections, thick vinyl can mask them. If a ceiling is low, covering the walls with a motif that has an upward thrust (such as a climbing trellis) will draw the eye upward.

Wood paneling comes in a huge range of tones, textures, patterns, finishes, and price ranges, and can run the gamut from rustic and casual to formal and fine. It insulates a room against heat loss, provides soundproofing, conceals uneven or crumbling walls, and can be recycled or newly installed. In a glassed-in room surrounded by trees, it can be used to forge a link with the scenery outside the window. In a room with an expanse of glass and stone, it can be used as an accent to add warmth. Paneling can be given a new look relatively easily with a different treatment—stain, glaze, or paint— which may also be used to address design problems. Boards or slats can be laid in a variety of patterns. Installing them in horizontal applications diminishes height and gives the illusion of width, while vertical applications do the opposite.

Tile makes as much sense in a glassed-in room as on a screened-in porch, since tile acts as a thermal surface that absorbs, stores, and slowly releases the heat from the sun in winter or the coolness from breezes or air conditioning in summer. Tile can make a major decorative impact since it is available in a wide range of materials, colors, textures, and patterns, and can be used to create patterns, motifs, or specific effects according to how it is installed. Tile can transform a room of little architectural or design interest into a dramatic space, or it can emphasize or exaggerate a room's dimensions. For instance, a horizontal band of color will give an impression of space, while vertical stripes will create the illusion of height in a low-ceilinged room. Tile is also durable and low-maintenance since it can be mopped and scrubbed.

OPPOSITE: *Tile and lattice-board are clever decorative treatments for this year-round porch, which is glassed in on three sides. The tile flooring absorbs, stores, and slowly releases heat from the sun in the winter, or coolness from breezes or air conditioning in the summer. The lattice-board provides soundproofing and adds an attractive decorative touch to the room.*

CRITTER CONTROL

While you want to keep some bugs out of your glassed room if you have plants, others are quite helpful at keeping the "bad" bugs away or removing them if they appear, though some can be quite expensive. The predator *Phytoseiulus persimilis* is a beneficial species of spider mite that will control the population of the unwelcome spider mites that eat plants. Or you can try misting the plant with rubbing alcohol, dabbing on the rubbing alcohol with cotton swabs, or spraying the plant with Pyrethrin. An effective way to control whiteflies is to introduce *Encarsia formosa,* a parasitic species of fly, into your greenhouse. Scale insects are difficult to get rid of because they're hard to detect. The best strategy is to scrape off or kill any crawlers as soon as

you spot them since the small crawling forms build hard shells over the plant that are impermeable to chemicals. Lacewings—which are inexpensive at about $7 for a thousand—will eat the insects when they're in the crawling stage but not once they hatch full-blown. Lacewings are also effective at controlling aphids.

These good bugs can be purchased through the mail from "bug stores," and many problems can easily be diagnosed over the phone by a bug expert, if you can describe what the invader looks like and if you know what plants you have. Keep a log of what you buy, since that's half the battle to making a good diagnosis, says bug expert Ken Miller of the Bug Store in St. Louis, Missouri. "A pest population grows in the absence of predators," he notes. Good prevention involves spreading eggs or releasing the good bugs over the winter months around your greenhouse or green room, as long as the cost justifies the means. If you have just one $5 plant and the predators cost $8, you may want to reconsider.

Other helpful tactics are to have bright light, which means at least six hours of southern sunlight daily; a humidifier when the house is dry; periodic misting; sufficient carbon dioxide (which is why some people think that talking to your plants is useful); low fertilization (since a few drops are healthier than a high dose); some circulation to dispel stagnant air and reduce diseases (which is why fans are useful); and judicious watering, since too much can be worse than too little. What's the right schedule for watering plants? Typically, twice a month for a large plant and every seven to ten days for a smaller plant. Excess water in saucers should be emptied. Finally, do the repotting in spring rather than winter, since plants like to be dormant and generally "sleep" rather than grow during the cold months.

LEFT: *Where a low stone wall once simply bordered an outdoor deck, the owners added glazing to create an indoor sunroom and painted the framing royal blue for a big jolt of color. Although surrounded by lush greenery, the plant life inside the room itself has been kept to a minimum to reduce the chances of insect problems.*
OPPOSITE: *Greenhouse rooms can be added almost anywhere that there is light, but a southern exposure will produce more blooms and help keep harmful insects at bay. Select flooring and furniture that will not be harmed by water or insect sprays— stone and teak are good choices.*

CHAPTER FOUR

Open to the World

enerally, the word patio conjures up the notion of a plain concrete slab projecting off the back of a house. A deck has a similar image, except it suggests a raised wooden platform instead of a ground-hugging slab. We usually imagine either one outfitted with a barbecue, a table, a few chairs, and a chaise longue or two, but that's about it as far as accoutrements go. We tend to think of these as fairly plain spaces, certainly not all done up with the same panache as a sunroom or porch.

But that image is far from the truth, for many patios or decks are anything but ordinary or routine today. These outside spaces have become total environments carefully designed by homeowners, often with the help of architects and landscape designers. Made of a variety of materials used in novel and creative ways, such areas are dressed with decorative furnishings, loaded with amenities, and surrounded by spectacular landscaping. They're much more than a bit of space outside the house; instead they have become an extension of our homes, offering room beyond the confines of our walls in which to relax, read, eat, entertain, enjoy the scenery, and even work, thanks to the mobility technology affords us today.

The benefits of a patio or deck don't end with these functions. If properly situated, designed, and executed, such a structure can be an optical enhancement to the whole back of a home, making the rooms that edge it seem more spacious. If a lot is quite large or awkwardly shaped, these structures can provide a graceful transition between the house and garden. In addition, a well-planned patio or deck can alleviate the burden placed on high-activity indoor rooms. Given all these advantages, it makes sense to assume that these structures can also increase the overall beauty and value of a home.

Whether you already have a patio or deck or plan to add one, a constant applies: it need be boring no longer. An existing structure can be renovated or revamped, while a new structure built from scratch can be tailored to the exact needs of your family and home. New designs, materials, and amenities abound to accomplish this task and make such spaces more comfortable, durable, and functional than ever before. However, figuring out how best to utilize these options can be daunting to the uninitiated. It pays to get some help when undertaking this sort of project, since it can get technical. Consider consulting or using the services of appropriate professionals, such as architects, landscape architects, landscape or building designers, general or landscape contractors, and structural and soil engineers.

OPPOSITE: *A patio can be much more—or less—than a plain concrete slab projecting off the back of a home. Consider a pathway that cuts through a yard, such as this one. Fashioned out of rich, rugged flagstone, it becomes a patio with the addition of a simple table and wicker chairs.*

Architects and landscape architects are state-licensed professionals who can see the whole project through from beginning to end, which includes designing the structure, negotiating with contractors, and supervising the work. For a far less substantial fee, they can be consulted on just the design of the project. Both landscape designers and building designers offer design and construction services; the former are not state-licensed, and the latter are either unlicensed or are licensed by the American Institute of Building Designers. Both general and landscape contractors should be licensed, and though some have design experience and are less costly than architects and landscape architects, they may also have limited design skills. Their strengths are overseeing, executing, and completing the construction on a project. Finally, structural or soil engineers may be necessary if the lot for the planned structure is unstable, steep, or exposed to unusual adversity on a regular basis due to the elements, such as high-speed winds or an exceptional amount of moisture.

Getting started is another hurdle that takes more research than meets the eye. Whether planning an overhaul of an existing structure or starting from scratch, it's important to consider a wide variety of issues, ranging from the design of your home and the size of its lot to the way you want to use the space and furnish it. Comfort, privacy, flexibility, durability, and safety are also important. Here are some parameters to consider.

HOME DESIGN. Even if the design of your home fits no specific category, it has a style that can be defined as casual or formal, it employs specific materials, and it has lines that define its profile (for instance, it may be squat and symmetrical or a rambling ranch-style). Assess these factors and determine what sort of patio or deck will best suit the style of your home. Try to tie the materials in to those already employed in the structure, and if this isn't possible, at least make sure that they relate in terms of texture or hue. Keep the scale similar as well; a huge sprawling deck off a small house will look out of place, while a small patio on a large home will look insufficient.

LOT. Is your lot large or small, symmetrical or lopsided, flat or sloped? Does the portion of it you plan to use for a patio or deck face north, south, east, or west? These are just a few of the questions to ask when planning this sort of structure. Lot shape and size govern the proportions of the structure, while the topography of the site dictates the physical design. A space that faces north will be cooler in every season because it will receive little sun; one that faces east will receive primarily morning sun; and a space oriented to the

94

south or west may get unbearably hot because it will get sun either most of the day or all afternoon.

~ *USE OF SPACE*. The way you plan to use your patio or deck is one of the most important factors to consider before building or revamping it. Will it be used for dining and entertaining, relaxing and reading, or as an extension of the kids' play space? With proper planning, a delightful dining area or a restful lounging space can coexist with a basketball or shuffleboard court. The structure can be built in levels, have low walls to separate spaces, or be a series of interconnecting surfaces. Start by making a list of all the activities you would like the space to accommodate, then use these as a basis to form a design plan.

~ *CIRCULATION PATTERNS*. Access to and from your patio or deck, and to portions of it if it's a multipurpose space, are critical to the way it will function and to how much you will enjoy it. Is the entrance to the space in a sensible spot, or will you have to walk through a room and interrupt an activity to gain access? Once on the patio or deck, does traffic flow smoothly or is it necessary to walk through the middle of a seating area to get to the barbecue or basketball court? Make a rough map of the structure, and pencil in its features (such as a barbecue, basketball net, or hot tub), activity areas, and furnishings before making final decisions about access and organization.

~ *PRIVACY*. Just like the rooms inside your home, a patio or deck should provide privacy. Without walls to block views, create boundaries, and seclude activity areas from one another, it's important to be creative. Where the structure is placed will impact this issue (a patio in the rear of a home will probably be more private than one off the side), as will the nature of the structure. An elevated deck, for example, might look right into an unsightly yard across the way, while a patio wouldn't offer the same view. Within the confines of the actual patio or deck, screens, arbors, and trellises can go a long way toward breaking up the space and providing privacy. They will also buffer noise and add to the beauty of the area if they are covered with foliage.

~ *FLEXIBILITY*. A patio or deck must be carefully planned to serve the ever-changing needs of your family. If it's to be used for entertaining and activities, the space must be versatile enough to accommodate both of these functions. This issue relates to the use of the whole space and its circulation patterns, but it can also be manipulated once plans are set. For instance, lightweight furnishings can be stacked on the side or

OPPOSITE: *The boundaries of this tiny stone patio are defined and privacy is created with simple and equally rustic elements, namely a wooden plank fence and two large slabs of stone.* ABOVE: *For privacy's sake, the deck that rims this home to take advantage of an ocean view has a series of architectural "loggias" to structure and define the space.*

ABOVE: *It is critical for furnishings on an open patio or deck to be comfortable, attractive, and able to withstand the elements. The simple lines of these pieces blend perfectly with the austere but elegant aesthetic imposed by the stone on this deck, and the furnishings are sturdy enough to be left out in rain.* OPPOSITE: *Pieces that are a little fussier need a bit more care, such as the protection provided by an awning.*

pushed out of the way; heavier pieces can be fitted with wheels. In a rainy climate, an awning that can be rolled up in sunny weather can enable the space to be used more often. In a very hot climate, a trellis covered with climbing flowers or vines can be used to cover and cool the whole space.

~ *DURABILITY.* A wide range of materials can be used to create a patio or deck, but no matter what you choose, it must be installed correctly and maintained properly or it won't be durable. If concrete isn't cured correctly, it can buckle and crack. Some tiles can crack in freezing weather (especially those that absorb water easily), or they may be a bit brittle and unable to handle accidental abuse (such as dropped objects). And wood needs constant maintenance; check for termites, and remove mildew, fungus, rust stains from nails, and large splinters regularly. Pick the materials you employ in the structure according to the constraints of your climate and how conscientious you will be about maintenance.

~ *SAFETY.* Take all safety hazards into consideration when planning a patio or deck. Some concretes, stones, tiles, and bricks become very slippery in wet weather, or are much too rough to accommodate children's activities. Decks that are elevated more than thirty inches (76cm) from the ground require railings. Hot tubs and deep fountains can be hazards to small children. The passage from your house to the patio or deck should be adequately illuminated at night, especially if there are any stairs to climb. And outdoor cooking areas should have fire extinguishers nearby, especially if they're on wood decks. These are just a few of the more generic concerns; every structure must be carefully analyzed to address all safety hazards.

~ *FURNISHINGS.* The rebirth of porches and related spaces has rejuvenated the outdoor furniture industry, so the options are virtually endless. A patio or deck can be outfitted with freestanding pieces, or built-in seating and tables can be used to gain more floor space. But remember to be absolutely certain that the pieces chosen to furnish these spaces are durable and completely weatherproof. For instance, rust can degrade wrought iron, while wood and textiles are subject to mildew, fungus, and decay.

A patio or deck designed to accommodate all of the concerns enumerated above will undoubtedly be comfortable. But such a space must be carefully conceived and meticulously executed. It takes planning, attention to detail, patience, and work, but the rewards are great. The result of all that effort will be a hardwearing, hardworking space that will serve the needs of your family and friends, enhance your lifestyle, and stand the test of time.

ABOVE: *With proper planning, it is possible to have it all. Here, an overhang covers just half the deck, a table can be moved underneath it for protection or away to enjoy the sun, and built-in seating can be used with or without the table.* OPPOSITE: *Sometimes the addition of just a few bold elements can make a patio more than the sum of its parts. Here, vivid flowering trees bring a simple patio to life.*

TYPES OF PATIOS AND DECKS

There are myriad incarnations of both the patio and the deck. Following are some of the types of structures to consider and tips on how they can fulfill your needs and be integrated into your property.

~ *BASIC SPACES.* A standard patio or deck doesn't have to be straightforward or boring. It can have contours and curves, several levels, or parts that are open or enclosed. It can be loaded with amenities ranging from a built-in barbecue to a gurgling fountain. It also need not be confined to the back of a home, for some spectacular and extremely useful spaces can be built on the side or front of a residence. Rooms that are located at the side of a home—such as a dining room, kitchen, or bedroom—can all be enhanced and expanded with a patio. A very public entry to a home can become a private oasis with the addition of a small patio arrayed with a

OPPOSITE: *Thanks to modern technology, a balcony can be laden with furnishings that are comfortable and elegant, yet withstand the elements. Despite appearances, everything from the sleek tiles to the cushy upholstery is weatherproof, and additional protection is afforded by a sturdy awning with a tubular steel foundation.*

fountain and a bench and enclosed with low stone or brick walls, a hedge, or an arbor.

~ *DETACHED SPACES.* A detached patio or deck can be built anywhere on a lot that is large enough to accommodate it. This type of outdoor space has one major advantage: since it's not connected to a residence, it can be started from scratch. But it is important to pay heed to the nature of the milieu; the style of the structure should relate to your residence and the surrounding grounds.

~ *INTERIOR COURTYARDS.* If an addition is being built onto a home, an existing patio can form the basis for an interior courtyard. Thanks to modern technology, it can even be capped with a motorized roof and glass walls that make it a year-round atrium.

~ *MULTILEVEL SPACES.* There's no reason to limit the contours of a patio or deck to a prosaic configuration, especially when a lot has an interesting terrain. Several patios can be built on ground that has changes in elevations, or both a patio and a deck can be employed, linked by a combination of steps and paths. This setup works particularly well in steeply pitched lots, where a variety of levels adds drama to the outdoor area.

~ *ROOFTOP AND BALCONY SPACES.* If you have a small yard and absolutely no room for a

patio or deck, consider building one on top of a garage or over a portion of your home, especially if it has a multilevel roofline. Balconies can also be added onto second stories, but an architect or structural engineer must be consulted to make sure that the structure can stand the weight of such an addition.

~ *SWIMMING POOL SURROUNDS.* If the focus of your yard is a swimming pool, build an entire recreational area around it with a patio or deck that relates to the area. This can enhance both the pool and your home by incorporating spaces that can be used for relaxing, working, eating, and entertaining. Some portions of the patio can be roofed to offer still more versatility.

~ *WRAPAROUND SPACES.* Houses that are situated on flat lots or have low, lean profiles are particularly suited to wraparound patios or decks. These structures can enlarge the appearance of the home and increase the living space of the rooms that border their contours. They need not traverse the entire perimeter; L-shaped or U-shaped structures are also effective.

ABOVE: *A shallow arcade goes from pretty to practical with the addition of a few comfortable pieces of furniture. The fact that it overlooks a spectacular pool increases the appeal of the space.*

OPPOSITE: *Thanks to the natural beauty of the seascape, this space doesn't need much to make it into an enchanting patio. The spare concrete table and handsome cedar chairs strike just the right chord in this setting.*

FURNISHINGS FOR THE GREAT OUTDOORS

When it comes to selecting furniture, nothing should be more important than comfort. But durability is also a major consideration for pieces that will "reside" outside. This type of furniture should be able to take a beating, because that's what it will get from the elements.

To obtain pieces that will truly stand the test of time in this sort of setting, and will offer up the kind of comfort you need to really relax and enjoy the space, it may be necessary to pay a little more. However, high-quality pieces that combine all these qualities will be both more economical and utilitarian in the long run.

For the most part, outdoor garden furniture is made out of wood, steel, aluminum, wrought iron, plastic, and resin in every style imaginable. Although the quintessential image of the porch calls wicker to mind, it's a material that's best left indoors unless it is the synthetic weatherproof variety. Options for furnishings range from antique and vintage offerings or historical reproductions to contemporary trappings of every ilk. A patio or deck can assume any style—from Victorian to Arts and Crafts to Spanish, Mediterranean, or even sleek industrial chic—depending on how it is furnished.

Some pieces are intended to stay out all year; others collapse, fold up, or stack for easy storage. Still other pieces are permanently built into the deck or patio, and are crafted out of the same sturdy materials of the structure itself, be it stone, brick, concrete, or wood. Most fold-up, collapsible, or stackable furniture is not meant to stay outdoors all year long or even in nasty weather. These pieces are not as heavy or durable as furnishings that are designed to withstand the elements, but they often don't cost as much either. Balance the cost against the performance required before deciding whether to splurge on more significant or durable furniture for an outdoor space.

Although plastic and resin can stay outdoors indefinitely, most garden furniture designed to stay outside all year is constructed of metal or wood that can really take a beating. Metals are often waterproofed and/or painted or enameled to withstand rust, while woods are either designed to acquire a decorative patina with weathering or are sealed with polyurethane. These pieces also tend to be heavier than collapsible or fold-up furniture—a testament to the way they are intended to be used. They won't blow away in the wind of a heavy storm, although it is necessary to close up umbrellas during severe weather regardless of how securely they are weighted.

It's often necessary to top outdoor chairs with cushions, and unless you have the perseverance to bring them in and out every time you use the space, make sure they're sturdy and weatherproof. To leave them outside, they need to be waterproof and mildew resistant. If they're stuffed with foam, there should be a "drainage system" to allow any moisture that has been absorbed to escape.

Here's what you need to know about the materials used for outdoor furniture.

~ *IRON.* Cast- or wrought-iron furniture is exceptionally heavy, which makes it ideal for windy climates. Unless it's an antique or art piece, it should be less expensive than aluminum but may require more care over time. Iron rusts relatively easily, and will need frequent paint-jobs and touch-ups whenever a new spot appears.

~ *ALUMINUM.* Also cast or wrought, aluminum is lightweight, durable, and rustproof, and it comes in a variety of textured and enameled finishes. Since these pieces tend to be more

OPPOSITE: *Outdoor furniture need not be fussy. Rather, it makes more sense to pick simple pieces and outfit them accordingly. These plain metal pieces are transformed by snappy striped cushions and a crisp white tablecloth.*

expensive, make sure the quality is there. Look for thick, heavy-gauge construction, smoothly welded seams, and above all else, comfort.

WOOD. There are myriad types of wood that can be used to make outdoor furniture, from cedar, redwood, fir, pine, cypress, or teak to pressure-treated lumber or plywood. Some varieties are naturally more resistant to decay and termites, such as cedar, redwood, and cypress, although they are a bit more expensive. Usually the better woods are left unpainted so their natural beauty will show. Painted woods usually require a yearly coat of paint and varnish (use products designed for outdoor use).

PLASTIC. Virtually indestructible, plastic comes in two forms: PVC piping that's joined together or resin, which is molded into a variety of shapes. Plastic also comes in many weights, so look for heavier pieces with smooth edges and sturdy construction.

OPPOSITE: *Time and again, it's easy to see why simple pieces work the best for outside spaces. Weatherproof wicker and wood can stay outside all summer, and be dressed up or down to meet every need. Here, the pieces take on a festive aura with a resplendent table setting.* RIGHT: *On a tiny front stoop, an Adirondack chair is all it takes to transform the space from ordinary to winsome and cozy. Thanks to the addition of the chair, the stoop now qualifies as a full-fledged front porch.*

ABOVE: *Most garden furniture designed to stay outdoors all year long is constructed of materials that can really take a beating. Though this dining set is exceptionally attractive, it has to be moved inside when the weather takes a turn for the worse. However, the heavy cast-iron garden chair in the background can stay out all year, thanks to its thick coat of waterproof paint.* OPPOSITE: *Simplicity reigns supreme on this patio, where the inherent beauty of two structural devices—namely a flagstone floor and a rough stone wall—takes center stage, thanks to the minimal furnishings. These two components also serve to define the space and give it a sense of structure in an otherwise open yard.*

PAVING MATERIALS

The material you use to fabricate a patio will have the greatest impact on the appearance and expense of the project. To make a choice, it is important to consider the properties of each material, the scope and budget of the project, and how the patio will be used. For instance, bricks can be employed to create richly textured surfaces in virtually any shape and pattern, and will not become excessively slippery when it rains. However, the bumpy surface is easier to trip on and is not conducive to kids' games or activities. Below are some of the options to consider when paving a patio.

BRICK. Since this is an ancient material that has had the same basic form and composition for over 5,000 years, it is not surprising that brick is available in hundreds of styles, colors, textures, and shapes today. It can also be used to achieve a great variety of patterns that range from simple to complex or traditional to contemporary.

Though there are many types of bricks to choose from at brickyards, the most basic types used for patios or paving areas in gardens are rough-textured common brick and smooth-surfaced face brick. The common brick is more porous, less expensive, and less uniform in size and color than face brick. It is most commonly found in three

varieties: sand-mold brick, which is slightly larger on one side and has rounded edges because it is turned out of a mold; clinker brick, which has a rough surface with smooth patches caused by overburning and gives a rugged cobblestone effect; and wire-cut brick, which is square cut and has sharp edges and a rough texture with pit marks. Face brick is smooth and durable, and produces a more even surface that can resist weathering but is very slippery. All outdoor bricks are graded according to their ability to withstand cold weather, so in areas

with severe temperature shifts, look for those graded SW (severe weathering).

There are no standard dimensions for bricks; they vary according to manufacturer, and even within each type or brand they are rarely exact or uniform in size. However, these discrepancies increase their charm and appeal, especially when they are arranged in specific patterns.

CONCRETE. Though it seems cold and unforgiving, concrete is actually more versatile than brick and can be used in countless ways. For instance, it can be textured, tinted, painted,

stained, scored, embossed, patterned, sand-blasted, acid-washed, embedded with other stones, or molded to resemble another material such as brick. To comprehend the breadth of these options, just imagine the textured approach alone, which can produce dozens of different decorative finishes by employing troweled, broomed, or pitted surfaces. It can also be stamped and/or tinted to resemble tile, stone, or brick. Best of all, concrete can be combined with other materials, such as stone, tile, and brick, or used as the foundation for a new surface of these materials.

Concrete is a mixture of Portland cement, sand, aggregate (usually gravel), and water. Sand and aggregate are fillers and control shrinkage, while cement is the glue that binds it all together and gives the mixture its hardness. Concrete comes in several forms, including dry ready-mix or wet ready-mix. It is also possible to order the components in bulk and mix them yourself for large patio projects, which makes the most sense economically. Bagged ready-mixed dry concrete is expensive but convenient for smaller projects, while wet ready-mix comes in a small

OPPOSITE: *Basic brick can be used to create a wide range of patio options. Here, it is employed to carve out a patio in front of a small storage shed located at the edge of a backyard, transforming the nature and utility of both the structure and the space.*
ABOVE: *Concrete pavers set in a harlequin pattern are an easy and economical way to create a stunning pool surround.*

trailer that holds one cubic yard (.77 cu m), is hauled by your car, and only has so much coverage (it can cover an area about eight feet by ten feet [2 by 3m]).

~ CONCRETE PAVERS. Forget the twelve-inch (30cm) square pavers that have been prevalent for years; today, pavers are available in many sizes, colors, textures, and shapes and are the ideal material for the do-it-yourselfer. These shapes, such as circles, rectangles, smaller squares, or hybrid configurations with faceted or serrated edges, can be made to look like stone, adobe, tile, or brick; are very easy to install; and fit together like puzzle pieces into mortarless, interlocking patterns. They can be used to create large, unbroken surfaces or can be spaced apart and interspersed with grass or gravel for a textured surface.

Although pavers come as thick as three inches (23cm), those between one and one-half inches and two and one-half inches (4 and 6cm) thick are fine for patios. They are cheaper and more durable than brick, and are now being made in varieties that have some wonderful variations of color and texture. If these aspects are important to your design, be sure to search out a variety that has color and texture embedded throughout; if applied only to the surface it will wear off.

~ CERAMIC TILE. With its earthy appearance and rich, warm hues, unglazed tile has a natural look that blends into many gardens. Glazed tile, which has a shiny hard finish and comes in much brighter tones, can also stand up to the elements and be used outdoors; however, it can be treacherous because the tiles are very slippery

shape because they are squeezed into forms under great pressure rather than molded. They also come in the same natural red, yellow, and brown hues as pavers. Synthetic stone, which is less expensive and more uniform in size than cut stone but has the same warm, natural appearance, usually mimics the look of granite or sandstone. Colors include shades of beige and a range of grays and blacks.

STONE. Stone is employed to create surfaces that range from rugged and rustic to smooth and sophisticated. Using it in irregular shapes and sizes can be a challenge, since it is important to keep the surface level and smooth, but many types of stone also come gauged, which means that they are cut to a specific thickness. Flagstone is technically any flat stone that is either naturally thin or has been split from a larger rock that cleaves easily; it comes in a wide range of colors and textures.

Flagstone varies by region, but basalt, bluestone, limestone, granite, sandstone, quartzite, and slate are commonly used for this sort of paving. When choosing a type of flagstone, think about how it will be used in your patio.

Stones with porous textures will absorb stains and would be poor choices for eating areas, and anything too smooth will be slippery when wet and so would not be ideal for a pool surround. Marble and granite provide the hardest surfaces; sedimentary stones such as sandstone or limestone are more porous and have a gritty texture but absorb moisture and can freeze and crack in a cold climate; and slate is a fine metamorphic rock which also tends to be slippery.

Fieldstone, rocks, and pebbles are less expensive than flagstone and can look quite elegant and charming, but also produce a very uneven surface. Smaller stones and pebbles can be set in mortar or in concrete. Many stones are available in precut tiles that have various widths and thicknesses. Slate, granite, sandstone, and quartzite are the most popular types of stones for precut tiles.

when wet. For this reason, unglazed tiles are a better choice for paving, and bright glazed tiles can be used for the decorative touches. Because all tiles (both glazed and unglazed) are fired, their pigments are permanent and nonfading and can withstand the elements.

Most outdoor tiles fall into one of three categories: pavers, quarry tile, or synthetic stone. Pavers are usually hand-molded and can range from rustic and rough to sleek and smooth in appearance. They are also generally earth-toned, ranging from yellow-orange to brown-red. Quarry tiles are usually smaller than pavers but thicker and more regular in

LEFT: *Classic ceramic tiles make an excellent material to use for a patio because they are durable, relatively economical, and come in a wide variety of earth tones that blend into many gardens. Rich terra-cotta pavers lend warmth to this expansive space.*
OPPOSITE: *Stone can be used to create effects that range from rustic to refined. Here, it proves the perfect complement for a Modernist house.*

CHAPTER FIVE

Special Places

Porches may be one of the most popular architectural additions used to enhance owners' enjoyment of their property, but numerous other outdoor structures and spaces are popping up on small and large city and suburban properties. This phenomenon is due to the increased interest (some would say obsession) that we have with gardening and spending time outside. Even though the energy crisis of the 1970s has not returned to any full-blown degree, that memory and the ever-present possibility of power shortages have encouraged more people to consider ways to pare their need for air conditioning by retreating to special outdoor spaces that take advantage of pleasant breezes, beautiful scenery, and sunlight.

Before you proceed to add an outdoor space that is separate or detached from your home, seriously evaluate your property's size and topography, and its pluses and minuses. You don't want to add so many structures that you gobble up open land and engulf your garden, trees, and flowers, all of which led you to consider ways to enjoy your site in the first place.

Next, consider your interests and how you can pursue them with a garden addition, which you should orient for the best light, shade, and views. Such an addition should always be constructed in proportion to the garden that it's a part of or closest to. The materials you choose to work with must always be suitable to your climate, the terrain, and the activity that will take place.

If you or other family members like to swim, you may want to construct a pool and a surrounding deck so that you can entertain outdoors as well as swim laps or frolic in the pool. If you like to play tennis, you may want to add the appropriate facility plus a shaded terrace for others to view the game or for you to relax after a vigorous match. If you're a boater, build a dock, boathouse, or nearby deck impervious to water and, if necessary, to salty and stormy air.

Gazebos, pool houses, playhouses, and freestanding greenhouses represent another genre—that of outdoor-oriented spaces that are more enclosed. They offer a special magic for quiet contemplation, a secret rendezvous, and make-believe play when grown-ups are nowhere in sight, or they may shelter a hot tub, lap pool, or orchid collection. Some pool houses in particular have become so elaborate that they might be better described as miniature homes, with fully functioning kitchens, living rooms, bathrooms, and sometimes bedrooms. Greenhouses can be ordered in kits or built to a custom design. Most additions

OPPOSITE: *A flagstone patio is recast as an architecturally significant site with the addition of a striking yet economical and utilitarian metal frame to surround it. For more drama and function, the frame can be covered with textiles in cool or inclement weather.*

are constructed with a choice of roof styles: an ogee, which is an S-shape crowned with a finial; a vault, which resembles a slightly arched dome; a classic gabled roof; or a hipped roof, with a gable that squares off.

Outdoor cooking has also evolved into a veritable art that far transcends the barbecue. Other options today include large-chamber smokers, stone hearths, brick ovens, rotisseries, industrial-strength woks, deep fryers, and weatherproof griddles and gas burners. And these outdoor cooking facilities rarely stand alone: a wide range of facilities such as preparation counters, storage cabinets, a refrigerator, a sink, and eating areas are often included in the mix, turning these spaces into outdoor kitchens that are usually covered with a roof or an awning. Often they are technological marvels, wired to the hilt for gas, electrical, and lighting needs.

Finally, don't rule out some outdoor structures that will provide a way to break up large expanses of lawn and serve more of an aesthetic than a functional purpose. Pergolas and arches fall into this category, creating wonderfully old-fashioned and sometimes romantic focal points of color, texture, and fragrance.

To begin planning your special space or spaces, think about your total site and how you would like to divide it into particular areas. If you have planted an exquisite French rose garden, you may want a simple gravel floor that gives the place an old-fashioned feeling, along with a comfortable bench or chair to provide a spot to relax with a good book. If you love to dine outdoors but want some shelter, you may be interested in a summerhouse that's open to the sun, stars, sky, and surrounding greenery yet affords some degree of privacy and coverage through the use of latticework covered with vines.

Whatever structure or design you decide on, be sure you select appropriate plantings, flowers, and trees to enhance it through a complementary mix of colors, textures, and heights. Also consider adding water in some form, either in a pool with some floating lilies or by way of a cascading fountain that cheerfully gurgles and ripples. You can gain additional pleasant sounds by hanging wind chimes or bird feeders that will bring delightful birds to your garden. You may also be able to install built-in water-resistant outdoor speakers so that you can play your favorite music. Satisfying all your senses is important if you're going to use your special garden spaces to maximum advantage and have others enjoy them as well.

Your outdoor space is also an idea spot for some artistic garden accessories such as urns, window boxes or planters, sculptures, statuary, and some elements that simply make it more conducive to relaxing. A large hammock (with a comfortable pillow) strung between giant oak trees works nicely for many, as does a swing big enough for two to rock gently.

There are many ways to customize outdoor areas to enhance their versatility.
OPPOSITE: *Consider breaking exceptionally large spaces into smaller activity centers. Here, the large surround rimming a pool has been divided into areas for sunning and dining.* ABOVE: *Latticework crowning an open-air atrium lends it a bit more privacy than if it were totally uncovered. Plus, the framework can serve as a foundation for foliage or fabric for additional coverage.*

ABOVE: *Wherever there are sizable supports, hammocks are a natural addition. Here, a unique, ultra-contemporary colonnade with massive columns fills the bill.* OPPOSITE: *An outdoor space is the ideal place for accessories that make it more conducive to relaxing. An ornamental pool in the middle of an open-air atrium is flanked by a table and chairs for activities such as talking, dining, or playing games.*

PLANNING THE SPACE

Deciding how you want to use your garden patio or deck is best done before you build it; that way necessities and amenities that can enhance its appearance and function can be designed and integrated into the plan from the very get-go. This approach is far more economical than going back and adding them after the project is completed. Here are some basics and extras to consider.

STORAGE. Almost everyone has tools and accessories that have to be stashed away when they are not in use. With careful planning, it's possible to hide them away close by so they're easily accessible when needed. For instance, the open space below a deck's foundation can be enclosed to make storage cabinets, or a hidden storage compartment with a trap door carved out of the actual surface of the deck can be built between the support beams or joists. Or, storage areas can be carved out of the perimeter of a deck by topping built-in benches with hinged lids. A garden shed, either hidden from sight or charming enough to stand on its own, is another option.

BUILT-IN FURNISHINGS. Built-in benches, with or without tables, often find their way onto patios and decks for good reason, since they are extremely versatile. They provide maximum seating in a minimum space; with the addition of cushions they can become more comfortable and attractive. Built-ins can also do double duty as buffets for serving food or shelving for showing off container plants. If furniture is added to the mix, they can become adjunct seating or serving spots.

PATHWAYS AND OVERHANGS. With the right attention, the passages or areas of shelter in a garden can be stunning and serviceable at the same time. For instance, pathways that connect the home or parts of a garden to the patio or deck can become extensions of the actual structure when made of the same materials or in the same style (paths leading from a patio can be made of brick or stone, while those from a deck can be dramatically elevated). Landscaping these paths enhances their appeal even more and raises the charm quotient of the entire garden. Overhangs can provide shelter and serve as an architectural enhancement to the space. They can be attached to a house or freestanding,

and can be built in virtually any style. For instance, lattice can be used to accent the patio area of a Victorian gingerbread house; a traditional Georgian home made out of brick may have an overhang supported by classic columns that shelters an outdoor space; or a sleek contemporary home may sport an equally sleek portico crafted out of steel grids and straight-edged concrete support beams.

WATER. Whether it's present in the form of a trickling fountain installed in a wall, a stream that meanders through the patio, or

a small pond filled with fish, water brings a soothing ambience to a patio or deck area. It is not difficult to introduce sources of water: some are as simple as filling a small portable pool-shaped container with goldfish and water plants, while others can be installed with flexible liners or fiberglass shells. These items are readily available in garden stores and are ideal for do-it-yourselfers. A formal stream or pond takes more work and may require the services of a professional, but can yield spectacular results that make it well worth the effort.

~ *BARBECUES, KITCHEN FACILITIES, FIRE PITS.* Outdoor cooking has evolved from the days of the simple grill. Today there are myriad options for the cook to consider, from simple fire pits ringed with logs or open-air barbecues, griddles, and burners to full-fledged, large-scale brick units that incorporate smokers, woks, and pizza ovens. A cooking area should be located conveniently close to the house, unless it also includes amenities such as a sink, a refrigerator, and storage for cooking and eating implements.

OPPOSITE: *An overhang can provide shelter and serve as an architectural enhancement to the space. Here, a latticework version grants a simple, straightforward deck a bit of shade and a good measure of architectural significance.*

RIGHT: *Many materials can be used to build a hot tub, but wood lends these structures a particularly warm appearance. It is important to sequester a hot tub from the rest of a yard for both privacy and safety's sake.*

It should also be at least partially covered by an overhang or gazebo; have ample and effective lighting; have all electrical outlets protected by watertight boxes; and be situated near a place to sit and enjoy meals.

~ *SPAS AND HOT TUBS.* Many materials can be used to build a spa that includes a hot tub, from wood and brick for a rustic or earthy appearance to stone or concrete for a contemporary or formal look. Ideally, a spa should be sequestered in a nook that will afford privacy and shelter from the elements with some kind of overhang. Seating around the area is also an important consideration; a stepped-down system of built-ins can facilitate use for the entire area around the tub.

You may want to have sufficient coverage above certain outdoor areas in the form of awnings, which now come in a wide array of colors, patterns, and materials, such as acrylic-painted army duck, acrylic-coated cotton, vinyl-coated cotton, vinyl-laminated polyester, and coated polyester, or giant umbrellas, which come in an equally diverse mix and often coordinate with tables and chairs.

Even though you're trying to get away when you go outdoors, it's wise to install sufficient outlets when possible, just in case you want to plug in a phone, your laptop, or a stereo or television.

Finally, before you're finished, you should incorporate some pathways, fences, and artificial lighting. The paths will provide important transitions between the various parts of your garden and your house, and the choice of materials should relate to the main home, even if the designs are not exactly similar. Some choices for pathways are brick, stone, gravel, or artificial materials. Fencing further defines the areas of your property, and it comes in innumerable styles to match your home—black Gothic-style wrought iron, a white wooden picket fence with a bit of a New England flair, warm brick that has a decided Southern edge, and rough stone that is reminiscent of the European countryside.

The Basics of Outdoor Lighting

Lighting should be bright enough to illuminate your garden and any special areas and structures, but should also be sufficiently crisp to light your house as the sun goes down. While some of the lighting should be functional—to keep visitors from tripping and discourage burglars—you'll also want some lighting to be decorative and add ambience. You can do this by grazing trees or by uplighting flower beds with tiny bulbs, or by installing wall sconces, dangling lights from the ceiling of a covered porch, or placing lamps and candles atop tables. Automatic timers can control lighting both indoors and outdoors.

Be aware that providing too much lighting not only ruins the ambience but also wastes energy. All lighting installation should be done before your garden and grounds are finished, since costs will increase significantly if bad planning forces you to dig up bushes and trees and replant them.

Protection from the elements can be an advantageous addition to an outdoor area, and it can take many forms.

OPPOSITE: *A metal overhang supported by concrete pillars proves to be the consummate chameleon. The top is tented and the sides are hung with crisp, striped cotton. The result is a well-protected patio that has a very sophisticated demeanor.*

ABOVE: *Here, an elementary lattice overhang is gussied up with plain white pillars and a chic complementary color scheme with dramatic results.*

125

Outdoor lighting is a necessity if you plan to use an outside space at night, whether it is a patio, deck, or separate structure situated in a garden. Just as it would be unwise to walk through an unlighted garden that may have steps or winding turns, it would be foolhardy to try to barbecue or swim without illumination. From an aesthetic standpoint, lighting will also add to the beauty of an outside space, emphasizing any unusual or interesting aspects of its architecture, design, or decor and creating a site-specific, mood-enhancing ambience.

Large areas with several different components to keep track of (for example, a deck with an outdoor cooking area and a pool) often demand expert treatment to maintain their functionality when it's dark outside, so get advice on these areas from an expert such as a landscape architect or lighting designer.

Following are some basic lighting considerations to keep in mind.

~ *LIGHTING SYSTEMS.* There are two basic systems to consider—the standard 120-volt system that is also used inside a home or a low-voltage system. While the 120-volt system can be used with standard appliances, tools, or space heaters and creates a brighter light that can be projected a greater distance, it requires a more complex installation with a buried cable and metallic fixtures. The low-voltage system is a popular option because it's safer, more energy-efficient, and easier to install, but it can be fairly expensive. It uses a transformer to step down the standard household current to just 12 volts. Though low-voltage fixtures are not nearly as bright as line-current fixtures, their output is adequate for most outdoor applications.

➤ *FIXTURES AND BULBS.* Most experts recommend first choosing the bulb you want and then picking the appropriate fixture to accommodate it. To choose a bulb, go for effect. Low-voltage halogen M-16 bulbs are popular for accenting, while PAR spotlights that come in both low or standard voltages are good for lighting trees or other wide-open expanses. A little light goes a long way at night, and 20-watt bulbs are considered strong. Opt instead for 12-watt bulbs, because lower-wattage bulbs have wider spreads. New fluorescent bulbs are also popular for outdoor use because their shapes and color rendition today are much better than in the past. Outdoor fixtures are made of aluminum, bronze, copper, plastic, stone, concrete, or various types of wood (redwood, cedar, and teak weather best). Sizes, shapes, and styles vary, but look for sturdy construction, especially at the pivot points, and locking devices for aiming the fixture.

➤ *BALANCE.* The view of a garden at night ends where your lights do, so take care to blanket evenly with light the areas you want illuminated, and check for black holes by surveying the entire area when lit. Lighting can also be used to break a patio, deck, or garden into clusters or zones by emphasizing certain areas, or even to create depth by giving specific zones more light than others (for instance, the background will recede with less light or serve as a bright backdrop with more light). Lighting must also match the activity: soft illumination is fine for conversation areas, but cooking areas will need stronger lights at night.

➤ *GLARE CONTROL.* Bright spots, hot spots, and unsightly glares that irritate eyes and leave afterimages can be a big problem with outdoor lighting at night because of the huge contrast between the darkness and the light source. To control these effects, use shielded light fixtures, which hide the bulb behind an opaque covering that directs the light away from the viewer's eyes and let the viewer see a warm glow instead of the light source. Place fixtures out of sight lines by positioning them either very low or very high and directing them so that light plays off something else, such as a wall or branches. Lower light levels by using many softer, lower-wattage lights strategically placed around a yard instead of a few high-wattage lights in one or two spots.

➤ *CONVENIENCE AND FLEXIBILITY.* If you want lights to go on and off automatically, consider having an electrician install some photocells and timers. The photocells go on and off depending on how much light is present or absent; the timers function on your predetermined time schedule. Many homeowners like

Any outdoor space gets much more mileage with an appropriate form of lighting.
OPPOSITE: *A patio used for dining benefits from a good lighting system. Here, a series of permanent lanterns gives the space elegance and a touch of romance.*
ABOVE: *Even an austere front stoop can become a more stylish and utilitarian area with the addition of lighting, which can be in keeping with the design of the structure, as these rustic fixtures of oxidized cordoned steel prove.*

to use both so that some lights go on automatically when it grows dark and others when the clock strikes a certain time. Opting for dimmer controls on lights and placing lights on separate switches also adds flexibility to the lighting system you install.

LIGHTING EFFECTS

Bulbs and fixtures work together to create dramatic ambient effects. Here's how to achieve each effect.

ACCENTING. Highlight a nook of the porch that has particular charm and appeal or a special spot, such as an ornately carved fountain, by placing several lights around the object or area to be highlighted, taking care to focus them directly on it. Balance them equally on either side, deciding whether to have them high, low, or evenly spaced depending on what's being highlighted.

BACKLIGHTING. Create a background that draws the eye to the far reaches of a boundary by placing diffuse lights behind a translucent material, such as a plastic or rice paper wall or screen.

GRAZING. Illuminate a stone wall, wrought-iron fence, or rugged tree trunk to bring out textures and shadows by mounting the fixture on the ground and shooting a beam of light parallel to the surface so that the beam grazes the surface.

MOONLIGHTING. Give the illusion of light radiating from the treetops by putting small fixtures in one or a few trees and pointing them earthward so that the light filters down through the trees.

PATH LIGHTING. Illuminate pathways, steps, railings, and walkways for safety and atmosphere at night. In this case, stick to 25-watt bulbs since smaller wattages don't light a large enough area. Mount fixtures twelve to fourteen feet (3.6 to 4.2m) apart.

SILHOUETTING. Create a bold, dramatic shadow on a smooth surface by placing a fixture directly in front of an object or skewed to one side for an interesting twist, pointing the light at the wall or surface behind to create a sharply defined shadow.

UPLIGHTING. Create an ambient glow that projects upward by mounting the fixture on the ground, preferably hidden from view, and pointing it up at an object, such as an overhang or a cluster of tree branches, that will catch the light and reflect it back down.

ABOVE: *A small covered porch in California's wine country is more of an outdoor living room with its floral upholstered wing chair and ottoman, an end table with a lamp, and a small dining table for late-night meals or a last cup of tea. The walls and roof were painted a picture-postcard blue, a good juxtaposition against the crisp white of the columns, balustrade, and louvered doors.*

OPPOSITE: *A simple setting can take on a whole new tone when it is bathed in the warm glow of candlelight at night. Here, a modest table and plain metal chairs become inviting and dramatic.*

LIGHTING LABS

If you're not sure what type of lighting to add to your garden and special outdoor rooms, there's a wonderful new option to help with your decision. Many of the seven hundred lighting stores that are members of the Dallas-based trade group the American Lighting Association have set up demonstration areas, or lighting labs, to show homeowners different types of indoor and outdoor lighting within the confines of the showrooms before they undertake major work on their houses.

In a lighting lab, which typically resembles a nice indoor room such as a kitchen or a pleasant outdoor space such as a garden, you can mix and match hundreds of different fixtures and lamps to achieve the right amount of light, the right ambience, and the right energy output.

The best demonstration areas are staffed by trained experts who can help you with an overall lighting plan. To take advantage of this opportunity, go armed with a plan of your garden, porch, or backyard (even if you only have a rough sketch); photographs of your home, of the existing terrain or room, and of any furniture you already own and want to use; measurements; the property's orientation (so that you know what area gets sunlight at what times); ideas of how you would like the garden and structures to look at different times of the day and night; and, perhaps most important, a list of activities you plan to do in that area. Cooking requires one type of light, reading another. Also clip pictures from shelter magazines of gardens that appeal to you, with any light sources in view. The more the lighting consultant sees, the more he or she can guide you to choose fixtures, lamps, and dimmer controls.

Some lighting showrooms offer such services for free while others charge an hourly rate that ranges between $35 and $50, which is typically reimbursable if you buy their products. Some lighting consultants will also make house calls. This service generally involves a fee of about $100, but again the fee is often reimbursable if you buy.

A large patio with an overhang needs appropriate illumination, even in the middle of the day. OPPOSITE: *Lanterns are mounted on the walls and hung from the ceiling of this stately portico to give the right amount and type of light to each of the various hubs of activity. Pale yellow walls reflect the light and soften the drama of the architecture.* ABOVE: *A series of Arts and Crafts–style lanterns provides the perfect touch of both style and service on this large patio.*

ABOVE: *An attractive table and chairs are sometimes all it takes. This charming spot would be appealing regardless of what the furnishings looked like, but the fact that they're pretty makes it even more stylish.* OPPOSITE: *There are many ways to dress up the everyday appearance of an outdoor space. A rooftop balcony with a loggia is especially nice to have since the overhead structure provides a basic foundation for any kind of decorative treatment. Adorn it with vines, and string lights for a special occasion.*

OPPOSITE: *A gravel driveway has been transformed into a casual sitting area, shaded by large trees and trained branches. The Adirondack-style furniture was found at a flea market and allowed to weather naturally. A white ironstone pitcher is continually filled with fresh flowers from the owners' garden.* ABOVE: *A tiny balcony with an exquisite view becomes an indispensable part of life with the addition of a humble chair.*

KEEPING PESTS AWAY

If you construct your porch or special outdoor space of wood—the favorite food of subterranean termites—be smart and take some preventive measures. Also be aware that other materials are part of the diet of certain termites, including the voracious Formosan feeders, who are happy to locate cracks to get through concrete and metal in order to get at any wood underneath the outer layers. They can destroy wood at five times the rate of regular termites.

Other unwelcome critters from which you need to protect your garden structures include carpenter ants and carpenter bees. The ants prefer softer woods with a higher moisture content. They don't actually eat the wood, but instead hollow it out to put their nests there. The bees are somewhat similar but are solitary critters that do not live in colonies; they burrow into the wood and lay their eggs there.

Before you build a porch or any other structure, have a professional exterminator treat the new foundation area with a chemical that repels or kills any unwanted visitors or helps destroy their nests. For those who don't want to treat their soil with chemicals, there's a new baiting system technology that allows homeowners to conquer subterranean termite activity using a bait that the termites carry back to their colony, which then destroys it.

To further avoid problems, seal any cracks throughout the foundation structure. Be sure that any wood elements are well above the ground so that you can periodically inspect them, and also be sure that wood does not come in contact with the soil, which makes it more susceptible to pests. Periodically—preferably once a year—have a pest-control inspector check your entire home for wood-destroying pests.

Signs of trouble are peeling paint, which may indicate a moisture problem, making the porch and other structures more conducive to infestations; holes in the wood not previously seen; and actual live or dead insects. Save some of the insects, and have them identified by your local pest control company. Be sure not to destroy all insects, since the "good" ones such as mantises and spiders attack the "bad" pests.

Also be sure to discourage any rodents from making your home their home. When enclosing a porch, it is essential to close all openings since these critters can squeeze through extremely small spaces. Also dispose of any uneaten food immediately rather than leaving it around as an enticement to vermin.

Finally, be certain that your porch, garden structures, and gutters have proper drainage, since pests are attracted to spongy or rotted wood.

ABOVE: *Despite the idyllic setting, there are hordes of unwelcome critters that can populate your outdoor spaces. Take precautions by protecting any and every garden structure. Have professional exterminators treat foundation areas before building your retreat, be it a simple patio or an elaborate deck.*

OPPOSITE: *Wood is particularly susceptible to a host of insects. Termites devour it, ants hollow it out to harbor their nests, and bees burrow into it to lay their eggs. Have an exterminator treat wood with chemicals that repel or kill unwanted visitors or destroy their nests. With these precautions, you can enjoy a beautiful all-wood porch, such as this one, for many years to come.*

GAZEBOS

In Victorian times, a gazebo was frequently included on a homeowner's property to add grace as well as to offer a private place for contemplation or a secret rendezvous. Typically constructed of wood, with eight sides plus a cupola-style roof made of cedar shakes or shingles, these free-standing structures have witnessed a resurgence of popularity because of their nostalgic charm and their flexibility. Screens can be added on the sides, as can glass; floors can be installed and even built off the ground with steps and legs to support them. Furthermore, many kits are available for handy and strong do-it-yourselfers who want to cut costs. (A gazebo with a diameter of twelve feet [3.6m] weighs about twenty-seven hundred pounds [1,226kg], so you will probably need a number of helping hands.)

Most gazebos are available in diameters ranging from eight to thirty feet (2.5 to 9m). The natural look is traditional, but they can be stained or painted almost any hue. If you opt for a design made from pressure-treated, kiln-dried wood, the wood will likely come with a lifetime warranty against rot, decay, termites, and fungal infestation. You may opt to treat the surface every few years since light and weather will gray the wood. Many gazebo designers and builders recommend staining rather than painting, since the stain penetrates the surface while the paint sticks to the surface and eventually chips or comes off. Costs vary, but a kit will typically run about $3,500; a finished gazebo stained white with a classic roof, a few steps, a floor, and installation averages about $6,000 to $7,000.

LEFT: *Gazebos come in myriad incarnations, and can revolutionize the entire nature of an outside space. A permanent structure with a sturdy foundation will stand the test of time, and can be screened or glassed in if desired for year-round use.*
OPPOSITE: *A clearing becomes far more significant and serviceable with the addition of an open-air gazebo. What better spot to enjoy the beautiful foliage and spicy scents of autumn?*

Appendix

Porch Terms

Before you make any decision about what type of porch suits you best, it's important to understand the options, as explained by the following terms.

Arcade: A line of arches and their supporting columns used as a passageway or an outdoor living space.

Balcony: An elevated platform that projects from the wall of a building, and is enclosed by a railing or balustrade.

Colonnade: A series of columns set at regular intervals, usually supporting a roof or series of arches.

Conservatory: A glass-enclosed room originally meant for growing or showing plants, but today often used by people.

Convertible: An open porch designed to convert to a covered or closed-in space if the season requires it.

Deck: A modern rendition of the patio, this platform occupies a whole or partial level of a home, juts into the landscape of the lot, and is usually uncovered, intentionally informal, and made of wood.

Gallery: Derived from the long indoor hallway in castles or palaces where portraits were exhibited, this also refers to a long, narrow balcony on the outside of a building.

Gazebo: A small, partially enclosed, house-like shelter, usually in the garden but sometimes attached to a house, in which case it is totally enclosed.

Greenhouse: *See* Sun space.

Loggia: An arcaded or roofed gallery built into or projecting from the side of a building, often on an upper story overlooking an open court and open on one or more sides.

Lookout: A small tower, usually on the roof.

L-shaped porch: A porch that wraps around the front and one side of a house.

Patio: Often paved, this ground-level space can be open or covered but always adjoins the back or side of the house.

Piazza: A covered gallery or arcade.

Portico: A porch consisting of a roof supported by columns, often at the entrance or across the front of a building. This romantic word derived from the Latin *porticus*.

Screened porch: A porch enclosed by mesh walls that help keep bugs at bay and offer some protection from the elements.

Setback: A porch, either open or screened, placed off the back of a house to provide a degree of privacy, protection from the elements, and a better view of the landscape.

Sleeping porch: A Victorian porch that originated in an attempt to cure tubercular lungs, this included a bed or couch on which to sleep or nap and was often built on the second story of a residence.

Stoop: A small porch or platform at the front of a house, with steps and originally with seats.

Sun space: Also called a sunroom or greenhouse, this highly stylized enclosed porch has a transparent roof and/or sides framed in wood or aluminum.

Veranda: An open porch or portico, usually roofed, that extends beyond a home's entrance and along one or more sides of a building; from the Hindi word *varanda,* and also spelled verandah.

Wraparound: A porch that wraps around the front and both sides of a home.

Window Terms

Homeowners should be familiar with these key window terms.

Acoustical glass: Laminated or insulating glass used for sound control.

Annealed glass: Glass that is cooled slowly to relieve internal stresses.

Apron: The flat piece of trim immediately beneath the sill of a window; also called a skirt.

Crown glass: An old-fashioned form of window glass, formed by blowing and whirling a hollow sphere of glass into a flat, circular disk with a center lump left from the worker's rod.

Dressing: The ornamental detail of a building, such as the molded framework around doors and windows.

Drip: Any of several devices that shed rainwater to prevent it from running onto the sill of an opening.

Drip cap: A molding that projects over an exterior window opening for catching and shedding rainwater.

Float glass: A flat glass composed of soda, lime, and silica that is the successor to plate glass and is manufactured by pouring molten glass onto a surface of molten tin and allowing it to cool slowly. It is extremely smooth and free of nearly all distortion, and accounts for the majority of all flat glass production today.

Glazing: Panes or sheets of glass or other transparent materials made to be set into window frames. (Double glazing is two parallel panes of glass with a sealed air space between to reduce the heat loss and sound penetration; triple glazing is three parallel panes.)

Heat-strengthened glass: Annealed glass that is partially tempered by the process of reheating and sudden cooling. It has about twice the strength of annealed glass of the same thickness.

Insulating glass: A glass unit constructed to retain heat, consisting of two or more sheets of glass that are separated by hermetically sealed air spaces.

Jamb: The vertical side of a window opening.

Laminated glass: Glass consisting of two or more piles of glass bonded under heat and pressure to resin interlayers that retain the fragments if the glass is broken; also called safety glass.

Mullion: A vertical strip that divides horizontal bars in a window, separating the glass into several sections or many smaller panes.

Muntin: A rail that holds the edges of the window panes within the sash; also called a sash bar or a glazing bar.

Obscure glass: Glass that has been etched with acid or sandblasted on one or both sides to obscure vision.

Patterned glass: Glass with an irregular surface pattern to diffuse light or obscure vision; also called figured glass.

Plate glass: A flat glass composed of soda, lime, and silica, formed by drawing molten glass through a series of rollers, which produces a plate that is then ground and polished after it cools.

Sash: The fixed or movable framework in a window into which panes of glass are set.

Sheet glass: A flat glass composed of soda, lime, and silica, made by drawing the molten glass vertically from a furnace. The surfaces are not perfectly smooth, resulting in some distortion of vision.

Tempered glass: Annealed glass that is heated and rapidly cooled to increase its strength and resistance. It has three to five times the strength of annealed glass when subjected to impact and thermal stresses, but it cannot be altered at all after fabrication.

Tinted glass: Glass whose chemical mixture absorbs a portion of the radiant heat and light that strike it; most commonly available in pale blue-green, gray, or bronze; also called heat-absorbing glass.

Window frame: The whole fixed frame of a window that is attached to the wall, consisting of two jambs, a head, and a sill.

Window unit: A manufactured unit consisting of the frame, sash, glazing, and hardware made to fit a window opening.

Source Directory

Decorative Accessories and Accoutrements

Casablanca Fan Company
761 Corporate Center Drive
Pomona, CA 91768
888-227-2178
Ceiling fans.

Design Toscano
17 E. Campbell Street
Arlington Heights, IL 60005
847-255-6760
Replicas of historical garden sculptures such as urns, angels, gargoyles, and the like.

Hunter Fan Company
2500 Frisco Avenue
Memphis, TN 38114
Ceiling fans.

Marty Travis
R.R. 1, Box 96
Fairbury, IL 61739
815-692-3336
Authentic-looking Shaker seed boxes.

Vermont Country Bird Houses
P.O. Box 220
East Arlington, VT 05252
802-375-0226
Handcrafted birdhouses with old-fashioned or unique designs.

Vintage Wood Works
Highway 34 South
Quinlan, TX 75474
903-356-2158
Wooden screen doors, porch doors, and decorative porch trim.

Furniture

Brown Jordan
9860 Gidley Street
El Monte, CA 91731
818-443-8971
Aluminum, wrought-iron, resin, and teak furniture and sun umbrellas.

Cumberland Woodcraft Company, Inc.
P.O. Drawer 609
Carlisle, PA 17013
800-367-1884
Resin Adirondack-style chairs and tables.

Ebel Inc.
3380 Philips Highway
Jacksonville, FL, 32207-4312
904-399-2777
www.ebelinc.com
Casual furniture suitable for outdoor use.

Giati Designs, Inc.
614 Santa Barbara Street
Santa Barbara, CA 93101
805-965-6535
Teak furniture, sun umbrellas, and exterior textiles.

The Lane Company Inc., Venture Division.
Box 849
Conover, NC 28613
800-750-5236
"Weather Master" wicker furniture.

Manmade
6988 Bayview Edison Road
Bow, WA 98232
360-766-8004
Handcrafted metal furniture and fences.

Marion Travis
P.O. Box 1041
Statesville, NC 28687
704-528-4424
Oak porch swings.

Michael Heltzer Furniture Design
4853 N. Ravenswood Avenue
Chicago, IL 60660
773-561-5612
Stainless steel and teak furniture with removable fast-dry cushions.

Metamorph
2700 Fourth Avenue South
Seattle, WA 98134
www.metamorfdesign.com
Recycled resin and plastic outdoor furniture.

Old Hickory Furniture Company
403 S. Noble Street
Shelbyville, IN 46176
800-232-2275
Rustic furnishings made of hickory, twigs, and the like.

Outdoor Lifestyle Inc.
918 N. Highland Street
Gastonia, NC 28052
800-294-4758
Leisure and outdoor furniture.

Pier 1 Imports
301 Commerce Street, Suite 600
Fort Worth, TX 76102
800-245-4595
Furnishings and decorative accessories for outdoor living areas. Check the phone book for a location near your home.

Triconfort
12200 Herbert Wayne Court, Suite 180
Huntersville, NC 28078
800-833-9390
Teak, lacquered resin, and aluminum garden furniture.

Winston Furniture Company
160 Village Street
Birmingham, AL 35124
205-980-4333
Casual furniture suitable for outdoor use.

Wood Classics
20 Osprey Lane
Gardiner, NY 12525
914-255-5651
Teak and mahogany outdoor furniture fully assembled or in kits.

Sunrooms, Garden Rooms, and Conservatories

Amdega and Machin Conservatories
3515 Lakeshore Drive
St. Joseph, MI 49085
800-922-0110

Four Seasons Sunrooms
5005 Veterans Highway
Holbrook, NY 11741
800-368-7732

Hartford Conservatories, Inc.
96A Commerce Way
Woburn MA 01801
800-963-8700

Screen Tight Porch Screening
System
407 St. James Street
Georgetown, SC 29440
800-768-7325

Sturdi-Built Greenhouse
Manufacturing Company
11304 SW Boones Ferry Road
Portland, OR 07219
800-722-4115

Gazebos, Trellises, Arches, Arbors, and Fences

Heritage Vinyl Products
1576 Magnolia Drive
Macon, MS 39341
800-473-3623
Maintenance-free fencing, decking, garden products.

Vixen Hill Gazebos
Main Street, Vixen Hill
Elveson, PA 19520
800-423-2766
Gazebos and screened garden houses.

Walpole Woodworkers
767 East Street
Walpole, MA 02081
800-343-6948
Handcrafted arches, arbors, and fences.

Catalogues Featuring Outdoor Furniture and Accessories

Crate and Barrel
800-323-5461

Frontgate
800-626-6488

Gardener's Eden
800-822-1214

Gardener's Supply Company
800-863-1700

Hen-Feathers Corporation
800-282-1910

L.L. Bean
800-341-4341

Plow & Hearth
800-627-1712

Resource Revival
800-866-8823

Smith & Hawkin
800-981-9888

Catalogues Featuring Plants and Seeds

W. Atlee Burpee & Company
800-888-1447

The Cook's Garden
800-457-9703

The Daffodil Mart
800-255-2852

Edmunds' Roses
888-481-7673

Geo. W. Park Seed Co.
800-845-3369

Greer Gardens
800-548-0111

Jackson & Perkins Company
800-292-4769

Milaeger's Gardens
800-669-9956

Seeds of Change
800-95-SEEDS

Wayside Gardens
800-845-1124

White Flower Farm
800-503-9624

Photo Credits

A-Z Botanical Collection Ltd.:
©Sheila Orme: 91, 138

©Philip Beaurline: 14, 19

©Antoine Bootz: 76 (designer: Cameron Nash)

©Fran Brennan: 55

©Derrick & Love: 18, 104 left

©Elizabeth Whiting and Associates: 5, 16, 20, 21, 22, 24, 27, 59, 63, 71, 81, 82, 83, 86, 90, 96, 97, 100, 108, 112, 119, 135

FPG International: ©Mike Malyszko: 25; ©Peter Gridley: 35

©Michael Garland: 131

©Steve Gross and Susan Daley: 2, 15, 29, 37; 41 (garden design: Nancy Mitchell and Marge Brower); 42, 53; 69 (designer: Randy Florke); 101, 122, 125, 129, 134, 139

©Nancy Hill: 58 (Furniture: Corner House Antiques)

Houses and Interiors: ©Mark Bolton: 61; ©Simon Butcher: 94, 110; ©Michael Harris: 68, 118; ©Steve Hawkin: 75

The Interior Archive: ©Laura Resen: 93; ©Schulenburg: 40, 49, 66, 87, 99, 102; ©Simon Sykes: 136; ©Woloszynski: 33, 56, 72, 78, 98

©Douglas Keister: 26

©Deborah Mazzoleni: 74 (designer: Fern Hill); 130; 137 (designer: Skip Siroka)

©Paul Rocheleau: 11, 12, 13, 44

©Eric Roth: 3, 23, 28; 31 (designer: Michele Topor); 57; 62 (designer: Jim Anderson); 64 (designer: Paul Magnuson); 65; 67 (designers: Domain Home Fashions); 70; 79; 84 (designer: Al Walker); 85 (designer: Gretel Clark); 109 (courtesy L.L. Bean, Inc.), 115 (architect: Edgar Tafel), 133 (designer: Michele Topor)

©William P. Steele: 52

©Tim Street-Porter: 10, 34 (designer: Tom Callaway), 73 (architects: Greene and Greene)

©Angelo Tondini/Focus Team: 17, 128

©Mark Turner: 43 (garden design: Renee Huizenga), 48 (garden design: Marie Smith), 123 (designer and builder: David Helm)

©Brian Vanden Brink: 47 (Bullock and Company Log Home Builders)

©Dominique Vorillon: 7, 9 (designer: Patrick Dune); 3; 50–51; 89; 95, 132 (designer: Paul Fortune); 104–105; 107 (designer: Stamps & Stamps); 111 (designer: Mia Lehrer); 113; 114 (designer: Nancy Power); 117, 120, 124 (designer: Moore-Bubbell-Yudell); 121; 126 (designer: Madeline Stuart); 127

Index

A

Apartments, 30, *31*, 60
Arcaded patios, *18*, *19*
Art Deco style, 28
Arts and Crafts style, 26, *73*
Awnings, *99*, *102*, 125

B

Balconies, 30, *102*, *135*
   rooftop, *31*, 103, *133*
Blinds, *74*, 80
Brick, 36, *37*, 85, 112, *112*
Built-ins, *17*, 122

C

Ceiling fans, *50*, 51, 56
Coir, 86
Colonial style, 12, 22
Color, 64–66, *69*, *81*, *87*, *128*
Community, porches and, 29–30
Concrete, 36, 98, 112–113, *113*
Conservatories, 60, 63, *84*, 87
   English-style, *70*
Cooking, outdoor, 119, 123
Cork, 39
Courtyards, interior, 103
Craftsman bungalow, *26*, 46–48
Curtains, 75–77

D

Decks, *40*, 92–115

F

Federal style, 12–14, *15*, *33*
Flagstone, 36, *111*, 114, *117*
Flooring, 36 39, 54, 85–86, 98
Furnishings
   arrangement of, 41
   built-in, *17*, 122
   outdoor, 98, 106–109
   wicker, 58–59, 106, *108*

G

Galleries, 12, *18*, 19, *19*
Gazebos, 116, 138, *138*, *139*
Georgian style, 12, 122
Glassed-in rooms, 60–91
Gothic Revival style, 19, 22
Gothic windows, *71*, 83
Greek Revival style, *11*, 19
Greenhouses, 60, 63, *91*
   freestanding, 116–129

H

Hammocks, 48, 119, *120*
Heating, 85
History, porch, 10–28
Hot tubs, *121*, 123, *123*

I

Insect control, 90, 136
International style, 27, 28
Italianate style, 19

L

Lanterns, *126*, *130*, *131*
Latticework, 28, 89, *119*, 122
Lighting, outdoor, 125–131
Linoleum, 39

M

Materials, 32–35
   curtain, 75–77
   flooring, 36–39, 85–86, 98
   furniture, 106–109
   paving, 112–114
   upholstery, 48–51
Moorish themes, *20*, *21*

O

Orientation, 32, 40, 54, 94–96
Overhangs, *100*, 122, *124*, *125*

P

Palladian style, 11, 12, 68
Pathways, 122, 125, 128
Patios, 92–115
Paving materials, 112–114
Planning, 40, 122–123
Plastic, 109
Prairie houses, 26–27
Privacy, 41, 97, 123

Q

Queen Anne style, 19, *23*

R

Romanesque Revival style, 22
Rooftop spaces, *31*, 103, *133*
Rubber, 39
Rush, 86

S

Safety, 29, 98
Screened porches, 46–57
Sea grass, 86
Second Empire style, 19
Shades, *76*, 77–80, *81*, *82*
Shutters, *64*, 80
Sisal, 85–86
Skylights, 54, *78*
Sleeping porches, 22, 35
Stick style, 22
Stickley, Gustav, 26, 46
Stone, 36, 86, 114, *115*
Stoops, *109*, 127
Swimming pools, 103, *104*, *118*
Swings, *43*, 48, *50*, 119

T

Tenting, ceiling, 82, 83
Tile
   floor, 36, *38*, *63*, 87, *89*, 98

paving, 113–114, *114*
wall coverings, 88
Tuscan columns, 14, *15*, 22

V

Victorian style, 19, 22, *24*, *25*
Vinyl, 39, 88

W

Wall treatments, 88
Water, 122–123
Wicker, 58–59, 106, 108
Windows, 68–71, 80–84
   decorative treatments, 74–80
Wood
   flooring, 39, 62, *73*, 98
   outdoor furniture, 106, 109
   paneling, 88
Wraparounds, *9*, *35*, *55*, 103
Wright, Frank Lloyd, 26, 27